Marching Nowhere

KEN HURWITZ

Marching Nowhere

W · W · NORTON & COMPANY · INC ·

NEW YORK

For my parents, my very best friends.

Acknowledgments

Special thanks to Star Lawrence for the time and patience of a good editor; to Lorna, a good typist and even better friend; and to Marty Peretz and Carl Brandt for the constant encouragement.

Marching Nowhere

CHAPTER ONE

Ye shall beat your swords on the Mississippi mud.
—GOD AND OTHERS LIKE HIM

Back in the spring of 1969 the world looked terribly bleak to the antiwar movement. It had been over two years since the huge march in New York of April 1967 and a year and a half since the October 1967 March on the Pentagon. The only major antiwar activity in the interim had been the disheartening and disillusioning McCarthy campaign. The great sadness of the time wasn't that the militarists and national chauvinists were increasing their numbers, but that the great masses of antiwar Americans had become so emotionally dismembered with the 1968 debacle that they were now mired in their own dejection. Many were beginning to learn to live with the war as if it were a type of smog, just another price for modern living. Like the rest, I too sat back and paid. And then came the spring, the girl, and the Moratorium.

It was the middle of May, and the fresh, sunny weather was making studying for exams a virtual impossibility. On my desk in front of me were a dozen books I had to read within the next week. Why? So I could prove to my professors that I had read the books, a tautology so simple that even I could grasp the absurdity of it. So prosaic was my academic life, I just didn't think about it.

Instead I thought about Marcie. For nearly four months I had barely heard a word in any of the lectures I had attended, and my reading comprehension was back to my level in third grade. I was paying two thousand dollars a semester to think about Marcie.

It was at the beginning of February that we met. I was the producer for a small-time college play, and she came to try out for the main female role. She was a sophomore at Wellesley College. It wasn't really love at first sight, which I've never believed in anyway. It was actually when she was still outside the tryout room and I heard her approaching feet that I knew for certain.

"My God, what a find you've made!" I exclaimed, slapping the freshman director on the back after Marcie had left. "That honey-colored hair, those intense gray eyes, that wit, that agile mind!"

"But the part calls for a West Virginian retard," the director objected.

"All depends on how you interpret the play. And if you still want to direct this play," I said in my most junior-to-freshman voice, "you might start thinking through your interpretation again."

"Gosh, I guess you might be right," he said. That half of the problem solved, I then suggested I take the role opposite Marcie. Like all intimidated freshman directors, he voiced no further objections.

And thus it came to be that Marcie and I spent seven weeks in rehearsal and production of William Saroyan's *Hello Out There*. I played a Texas dude who got to kiss the girl twice before being shot dead, a more than fair exchange as far as I was concerned. By the middle of March I knew my instincts had been correct and that make-believe love was being woven into the real thing.

Over those next spring months we did nearly everything together. We hitchhiked from Boston to Columbus, Ohio, to spend a weekend with her flabbergasted parents, went on picnics to New Hampshire and Cape Cod, played frisbee along the bank of the Charles River, splashed through the melting snow and early spring downpours, laughed at her ugly, floppy rain hat, played tennis until I discovered she could beat me, wrestled until she discovered I could beat her, laughed at my turned-out ankles, and just simply fell in love.

I offered no resistance to my emotions. Before Marcie, I had feared only that perhaps this kind of overwhelming feeling of tenderness, this sensation of selfless caring would never be a part of my life. There had always been girls to date, but that's where it had always remained, at "dating." Never before had all those defenses come tumbling down until I could see the whole of tenderness I never even knew I possessed. The first involve- ment—I cheered the current that towed me under.

It was in that same spring, however, while my personal life was swimming, that politically I was becoming more and more agitated. Only five weeks earlier had been the bust and strike at Harvard. SDS had gone into University Hall because of ROTC; the cops went into University Hall because of SDS. A few days later I found myself at the football stadium, voting along with thousands of other students in favor of a strike.

When the late-afternoon rally concluded, I carefully fastened my red armband and walked through the long shadows being cast by the stadium pillars, heading slowly for my room in Leverett House. A warm and gentle spring day was coming to a finish, but inside me was a gnawing and unsettled feeling. Somehow things weren't right. I wasn't fitting in where I wanted

to fit. I was against the war—as much against it as anyone—
but what was I doing about it? As a so-called moderate student
I was waiting for groups like SDS to take the initiative, to create
an event that would force me to choose between them and the
"other side," the ones who called in the police. Like many, I
had voted for a strike mainly because of the untempered brutal-
ity of the police bust, but beyond that there was no real choice
for me.

The SDS views simply were not my views. Like so many
other students I knew, I was caught in that great, guilt-corroded
limbo between liberalism and radicalism, sometimes called left-
liberalism. Certainly, I could accept a great portion of Marxist
analysis of the interplay between economics and politics, and I
knew I could live quite contentedly in a socialist state. But seeing the virtues of socialism while at the same time still believing
in the viability of a controlled capitalism left me a good margin
removed from my friends and even roommates in SDS, who
believed that the revolution would not only bring forth economic utopia, but would solve every other human problem as
well, the war just for openers. I remained skeptical. Communist
countries themselves offered too much evidence that racism,
militarism, and all the other pernicious *isms* are a function of a
thousand different social factors, not just the ownership of
production.

And beyond *those* differences I held with SDS, there was
always the question of tactics as well. Though the D in their
title stood for *Democratic*, it was clear there was nothing more
to that claim than pretence. They spent half their time shouting
down speakers who they had decided didn't have the "right" to
speak, and making it clear in other ways that the majority (which
just wasn't fortunate enough to have a "true class consciousness") would have to be coerced. What they accepted in people
like Mao—and which they usually termed "democratic *central-
ism*"—they certainly would brand elitism, if not totalitarianism,

were it to exist in American government. As long as it was in the cause of socialism, it was justifiable. That kind of suspension of democracy I simply couldn't accept. It had already led too many Americans to believe that communism necessitates totalitarianism, which it of course does not.

And the basis of all their rhetoric was the cry for revolution. Just mention of the word put a glint in these upper-middle-class kids' eyes. REVOLUTION—it seemed to inject romanticism into their otherwise bored and humorless lives. We would all be Errol Flynn, but instead of holding knives in our teeth we would all have machine guns, laughing and riddling our favorite parents and deans. I simply couldn't believe how lightly many of them took the word, how naive they were to the realities of an actual revolution. *Cultural* revolution and I have always been friends, but what about one that was predicated on the deaths of several million people? How could they talk so nonchalantly about organized violence? To me, it didn't matter which flag would fly over the corpses.

No, I really couldn't be a part of groups like SDS. But who then could I side with? The Harvard Administration? As far as I could see the Harvard Corporation's duplicity with the students was matched only by its complicity with the military. No matter how it pleaded political disinterest and academic neutrality, the university's weapons research and the privileged status of ROTC clearly aided the war effort. Side with them? No, thank you.

And so the days and weeks passed while I did nothing and felt an affinity for no one. Every night Marcie and I watched the evening news, saw the films of the bodies, heard the weekly figures. I couldn't blame Walter Cronkite for the emotionlessness of his voice each time he announced new casualties. How could he or any of us comprehend the entirety of what was happening? Without our psychological defenses we can't survive. Only the summer before, a friend of mine had been killed in a hiking accident, and for the first time I came to understand the sorrow in a young person's needless death. For the first time I was witness to the months of anguish for a family and friends. How then could any of us truly comprehend the horror of several thousand young people dying each week in Vietnam? To know that kind of *Weltschmerz* is to be cursed. No, I couldn't blame the newscasters. They too had a sanity to preserve.

But sanity may be all that is preserved. Every night the news—and every night I slipped further into a depression of helplessness. I railed against the war and yet criticized my SDS roommates for any of the antiwar actions they took. Marcie, as nearly apolitical as she was, saw as well as I did what it was doing to me.

"Honey, you can't just keep doing this." She was chastising as much as pleading. "Why don't you go see those people at the Friends' Committee, or *someone?*"

After a few more weeks of unproductive thought on the matter I took my problem to one of my roommates, Bob Krim, who was the *Washington Post* stringer in Cambridge and was in touch with many of the planned antiwar activities around the country. Being of a more radical bent than I, he couldn't appreciate my exact political position but was willing to help just the same. As he leaned back in his chair and removed his wire-rimmed glasses to better reveal his anti-liberal grimace, he suggested I go see Sam Brown about "that Moratorium thing of his."

This in fact was just about the state of affairs of the Moratorium at the time—an amorphous "thing," no organization, just an idea and a rough one at that. Its history up until that time had been a short one. It began in April at a meeting of Mass. PAX, a Massachusetts peace organization. At that meeting Jerome Grossman, chairman of PAX, suggested the idea of a "general deadline strike" to commence some time in the fall. After the meeting Marty Peretz (an assistant professor at Harvard, and my tutor and thesis advisor for two years) and his wife, Anne, took the idea to their friend Sam Brown. Brown talked it over with other organizers as well as with undergraduates in the seminar he was teaching at the Kennedy Institute of Politics.

Many of the eventual refinements of the concept were in fact first suggested during these seminar discussions. One was to change the word *strike* to *moratorium* so as not to imply an action against the institution (e.g. school, factory, store, or the like) rather than an action against the government. Another problem with *strike* is that it connotes forcible, not voluntary, work stoppage, an obvious disability in trying to appeal to a moderate constituency. Also it was suggested that instead of hoping for a complete lay-off, it would be wiser to expand the Moratorium one day each month, starting the movement on campuses, where it would receive its greatest support, during the first month.

Bob Krim set up a meeting with Brown for me, and two days later I was walking along the cobblestoned sidewalk of Mount Auburn Street to the Kennedy Institute of Politics. All I really knew of Brown was what I had read in the papers. It was one of those conservative-to-activist stories. Son of a wealthy Council Bluffs, Iowa, businessman; went to Redlands University, where he was not only student-body president, but also— and I whisper it—president of the Young Republicans; then, as his politics began changing, helped organize the Dump Johnson movement as vice president of the National Student Association; then in 1968 became the national director of the Youth for McCarthy—he was the children's crusade's "chief kid." Because of the campaign Brown had dropped out of Harvard Divinity School, which he was then attending, and when it was all over he became a Fellow at the Kennedy Institute.

As I neared the little yellow wooden building that looked more like one of Frost's New England houses than an institute,

I tried to prepare myself for any eventuality in the conversation. Pausing on the shaded porch outside the front door, I quickly reviewed any initials of organizations he might throw into the conversation—SCLC, AFSC, FOR, NDC—*Bill* meant William Kunstler, *Al* meant Allard Lowenstein, et cetera, et cetera. When I felt ready I went in.

Just inside, the receptionist told me that his office was on the second floor and that he was expecting me. With renewed confidence I bounded up the banistered stairway, gave a tug on my shirt sleeves so they'd hang longer than my sportcoat, and presented myself in the open doorway to his office.

"Sam?" He was only twenty-five—what the hell.

A slender young man with a puckishly innocent smile rose from his typing to greet me. The sleeves of his pin-striped shirt were rolled up like any good organizer's, and his mile-wide, flowered tie swayed freely from his loosened collar. I took my seat and he took his, but not before getting a firm grasp on his doodling pen. You learn quickly that if Sam doesn't have a pen with which to draw and gesture, you had better supply one if you expect to get down to any serious conversation. Aside from his youthfully shaggy hair, another change from Sam's "Clean for Gene in '68" look was his drooping walrus mustache. After about three seconds of conversation he suggested we go downstairs for some coffee.

A minute later we were sitting comfortably in the first-floor living room of the Institute. While Brown relaxed on the couch in front of the fireplace, I sat upright and a bit nervously in a leather chair on the other side of the coffee table. Facing the front door, I caught a glimpse every now and then of familiar government professors going in and out of the Institute, all looking more genuine and at ease than when behind lecterns. Sam was telling me that this was already his sixth or seventh cup of coffee that morning, a common hazard of antiwar organizing. Then we got into the Moratorium. He spoke softly as he rolled the pen between the palms of his hands.

"You see, it's not just a small group of tired old "peaceniks" or fringe percentage of radicals that are willing to protest the war. It's millions of people in every part of the country, even places like Mississippi—all they need is a little push and the right channel."

He didn't have to tell me—I was one of them.

"Now I'm not saying," he continued in his soft but sanguine voice, "that between now and October 15 we can educate masses of people who are still *for* the war as to why this war's an atrocity. That kind of education takes time. But we *can* mobilize the people that are already against it. And if we do our job right there's no reason we can't get millions of people to stop working in protest. We can make it damn hard for Nixon to continue this war. I've spent a lot of time traveling around the country—you just have no idea how many people are ready now to do something about the war."

It was nearly impossible to not get caught up in his optimism and enthusiasm, and I wasn't trying to fight it. He leaned forward to take another sip of coffee, but his mustache got most of it.

"And *my* job?" I asked.

"Well, while some of the rest of us start working on congressmen and unions and groups like that, you and a couple others will get the organization going on the campuses. It'll be a lot of phoning and probably a fair amount of traveling too."

I leaned forward over the coffee table and with a rising air of confidence and belonging shook the sugar to the bottom of its bag container. "Where is all the money going to come from?"

"Yeah, that's going to be my job," he answered. "We should be able to get a fair amount from the old McCarthy

contributors." Then with a wink, "Especially our mutual Cambridge friends." That meant Marty and Anne Peretz, who had
been giving generous sums to left-liberal causes for some years.
"I'll get an idea of how much in the next couple of weeks."
He paused and then added somewhat apologetically, "But that
brings up another point—all of our salaries will be pretty much
subsistence level."

That was of course perfectly all right with me. I really
wasn't expecting any stock options. The next forty minutes or
so were taken up by my questions concerning the specifics of
how one goes about organizing campuses. It wasn't easy asking
what to do without sounding like I didn't know what to do.
The bullshit I threw in between naive questions wasn't enough
to impress even me, but just the same, Sam told me to come
down to Washington some time during the first two weeks in
June and I could begin working.

Once outside the Institute, I loosened my tie and tossed
my sportcoat over my shoulder. The whole walk back, my spirit
wagged between complete belief in this new idea called the
Moratorium, and total doubt. Optimism, skepticism, optimism,
skepticism—the ebb and flow of a beginner. As I neared
Leverett House I was on the upside of the teeter-totter when I
passed an old friend from freshman year.

"Hey, Ken. What are you doin' this summer?" he called
from across the street.

"Going down to Washington to end the war." I called
back.

Once back in my room Locke and Rousseau seemed even
more useless than before, but somehow I managed to get
through them *and* my exams. Several weeks later I was on a
plane to Washington, D.C., and a day after that I was riding
up an elevator in an old downtown Washington office building.

As the elevator made its slow ascent I could feel another
bead of sweat begin to form along the side of my nose. Just the

fifteen-minute walk from the house had turned my shirt and pants to Saran Wrap. The dingy-brown fanless elevator chamber continued up the numbers, and I continued to wish I were on a plane for Europe. That's where Marcie was and would be for the rest of the summer. She had said that being separated would be good for us because it would reaffirm her independence, which she said she still needed. If it was so good for us, I had asked, why did we both cry for three hours before going to the airport? She didn't answer that—she only started crying again.

Number 4, then 5, then 6. It was June 16—more precisely, June 16 in Washington, D.C., which meant it was about ninety-seven degrees, with the humidity at least that. I was wearing what was to become my daily business suit—open-collar sport shirt, filthy khaki pants, moccasins, no socks.

As number 7 made its brief appearance I pulled from my pocket a folded, soggy piece of paper. I opened it and read it again to be sure—"1029 Vermont Ave., Suite 806." So this is where we're going to organize the Moratorium from, eh? Close the nation down, eh? This would be a good building to start with. At the eighth floor the elevator came to a gentle stop and I stepped out into a dark and narrow hallway.

The light in 806 was on and shining through the frosted glass door. With a pearl diver's last big breath I stepped through the threshold of our new headquarters.

Headquarters? As the fluorescent light above flickered I stood in the open doorway, my death gaze covering the large, barren room from one end to the other. In front of me were three splinter-painted doors leading to three smaller rooms. The unwashed brown floor held no chairs, desks, or tables— only dust and several dangling telephone wires that were yet to be connected. The dirty beige walls were empty, and in places the plaster was buckling.

But political visions can work wonders. The ability to periodically dismiss reality is the organizer's most necessary prerequisite. *Click*—I looked again and saw dozens of secretaries rushing about to answer the hundreds of incoming calls, the barrage of flashes from reporters' cameras, messengers at the door with telegrams of congratulations from U Thant, the Pope, Natalie Wood. I saw Moratorium balloons everywhere, Creighton Abrams standing in the corner wearing a Moratorium button, Nixon on the phone pleading for mercy. *Click, click.* I saw a dirty brown floor, empty beige walls, and a few dangling telephone wires.

As I ventured in a few steps, my ear was caught by the strained whistling of "I Ain't Marching Anymore." It was coming from a fourth adjoining room that I hadn't noticed when I first came in. Its door was closed.

"Hello?" I called.

The whistling stopped. And in a moment I heard the rustling of someone getting up off the ground and coming in my direction. The door opened and a head with curly black hair and a neatly trimmed, curly black beard popped out.

"Hi, I'm Dick Lavine." He came over to me with his hand extended. "There are about as many chairs in there as in here," he laughed as he brushed off the seat of his pants. He sized me up through his black-rimmed glasses, and I did the same for him. Our mutually familiar faces were explained by the fact that Dick had just graduated from Harvard, where he had known Brown through the seminar at the Kennedy Institute. We immediately took to each other and talked for some time about shared friends in Cambridge. I liked his manner. It was easy and jovial, even though his gyrating arm gestures suggested the coming of the end.

Then Dick showed me around the rest of the office, noting that single-line phones had been installed in three of the four smaller office rooms, and that air conditioners would be in by the next day. "Bless you," was all I could think of to say.

After the tour there was nothing more to do other than

wait for Sam, who would be coming within the hour. I sat on the floor of the large outer room leaning against the wall, a section of the *Washington Post* that Dick had given me across my lap. A lead article said that infiltration into South Vietnam was up by 1,064—they must have turnstiles at the border.

Just as I was getting to the news about the ABM and pictures of David and Julie giggling at some White House affair, Sam came in along with Dave Hawk, another of the Moratorium's main coordinators. Hawk had been working for the past year with the National Student Association as head of that organization's antidraft campaign. Several months earlier he had organized over 250 student-body presidents and college newspaper editors in signing a "We Won't Go" letter, and before that he had made the news as an indicted draft resister from Union Theological Seminary. His blue suit hung loosely on his athletic build—he was formerly an All-American diver at Cornell—the picture of an athlete turned organizer as he put out one cigarette and lit another. He viewed me through his wire-rimmed glasses with that intense look of his, and I was reminded of the revolutionary intellectual Strelnikov, in *Doctor Zhivago*.

The immediate goal was to collect one hundred endorsements from college student-body presidents and newspaper editors within the next two weeks before Sam's planned June 30 press conference. It's not that student-body presidents are campuses' best organizers or are the most politically astute, but from a pragmatic viewpoint, it's just a fact of campus life that the large masses of students are far more likely to participate in a protest that is endorsed and at least partially organized by the student government, than if the organization were totally in the hands of a smaller, radical group on campus. This isn't to say that radical groups were discouraged in any way from helping, but only that it was important to insure that at least part of the local organizations were composed of more moderate people. They would set the terms—radicals could join or stay clear, as they saw fit. Also, when dealing with the press it never hurts to have the student presidents' and editors' endorsements on hand. There wasn't time, however, for a mass mailing, and so this first set of endorsements had to be obtained by phone with the help of Hawk's list of "We Won't Go" signers.

Sprawled out over the floors of the five rooms, we used the single-line phones that were already installed to begin the phoning that night. The first name I picked was that of the student-body president at Texas Lutheran. After about five calls to trace him to his summer phone number I finally got hold of my man.

"Hello, my name is Ken Hurwitz. I'm calling you for the Vietnam Moratorium Committee. We're a new organization that has just set up offices in Washington, D.C., to begin organizing a national protest against the war in Vietnam. If you think you might be interested in helping, I'd like to read you a statement of our purpose and ask you for your endorsement."

"Ya damn raht ahm interested," came the southern drawl. "Go 'head an' shoot" (an untimely metaphor).

"All right, here it is." I then proceeded to read him the following "Student Call" that had been written earlier in the spring by Sam and a couple of his colleagues:

"Ending the war in Vietnam is the most important task facing the American nation. Over the last few years, millions of Americans have campaigned, protested, and demonstrated against the war. Few now defend the war, yet it continues. Death and destruction are unabated; bombs and fire continue to devastate South Vietnam."

Over the next ten weeks I would be reading those lines again and again. I hated it. There was no way to read them over and over without sounding formulated, political, cold.

"Billions of dollars are spent on war while the urgent domestic problems of this country remain unattended. Moreover, the war

has had a corrupting influence on every aspect of American life, and much of the national discontent can be traced to its influence.

The discredited policies of the past which have brought about the American tragedy have not been changed. We follow the same military advice which has created a futile and bloody conflict while we cling to the same policies which have caused the Paris negotiations to falter. The token displacement of twenty-five thousand troops over a three-month period is not the substantial change in policy that is so desperately needed.

Thus it is necessary for all those who desire peace to become active again and help bring pressure to bear on the present administration.

We call for a periodic moratorium on 'business as usual' in order that students, faculty members, and concerned citizens can devote time and energy to the important work of taking the issue of peace in Vietnam to the larger community.

If the war continues this fall and there is no firm commitment to American withdrawal or a negotiated settlement, on October 15 participating members of the academic community will spend the entire day organizing against the war and working in the community to get others to join us in an enlarged and lengthened moratorium in November. This process will continue until there is American withdrawal or a negotiated settlement.

We call upon all members of the university community to support the moratorium, and we commit ourselves to organize this effort on our campus and in the larger community. We ask others to join us."

"Raht on, Ken! Ahm with ya all the way."

"Good enough. Then I can use your name?"

"Ya betcha, and ahl 'spect to hear from ya again real soon."

"Sure thing," I answered. "'Bye now." I hung up the phone and turned to Hawk. "Wahl, bless mah dogwood. This ain't hard 'tall."

"Don't get too excited yet." Dave said as his cigarette bobbed up and down between his lips. "Remember, these are the people that already signed the 'We Won't Go' letter. If they're not with us, no one is." I was beginning to wonder if Dave ever smiled.

I put a check mark next to Texas Lutheran and turned to the next card, a college newspaper editor somewhere in Pennsylvania. He had a little trouble hearing me read the statement over the party in the background (his party, not mine), but as long as it was antiwar, he was for it. Another check mark— I continued down the list. By this time one of my summer roommates, Peter, had come over to the office to help. He had plans to work in Senator Ribicoff's office for the summer but didn't have to start work for a couple of days. I gave him a few of my cards, and he began calling from one of the other rooms. Next I called the student-body president from some junior college in Illinois. He wasn't home, but unfortunately his mother was.

"Freddy's not home. Who can I say is calling?"

"Sir," the operator interceded, "The party isn't in. Would you like to leave a message?"

"Yes, tell him that Ken Hurwitz from the Vietnam Moratorium Committee called, and that he should call me collect when he gets in."

"Ma'am," the operator said, "have the party return the call collect to Ken Horowitz at the Vietnam Mortuary. The number is——"

"No, no. That's Ken Hurwitz and it's the Vietnam *Moratorium* Committee."

"Freddy doesn't know anyone like that," his mother interjected. "Is this Billy Ferguson with another one of your prank calls?"

In the meantime the operator was still trying to get the names straight. "That's Vietnam—what?"

"Moratorium, operator. M . . . O . . . R . . . A . . .
T . . . O . . . R . . I . . U . . . M."

"Is this the same group that made Freddy sign that fool
letter about the draft?" his mother asked.

"Look, lady, no one *made* your son sign anything."

By this time the operator, who was at the end of her
cracker, said she'd have to cut off the conversation, considering
that the party wasn't even in. That was all right with me—
I'd call him at his school number. The mother was telling the
operator something about "flag-burners at Munich" when I
hung up the receiver.

I sat at the phone for a couple of minutes exuding silent
anger. I was getting my first taste of frustration over those
"other people" in the world. Sure, I had been with people before who I had thought were unreasonable and uninformed,
but before I could always dismiss the differences. "You can't
change everyone." They'd go their way and I'd go mine. You
can always do that when the conversations are mere bull sessions. But now these people represented a very real obstacle to
something I was trying to achieve. It was no longer just a matter
of debating. And it made me angry. But don't get angry, I
thought. These are the people we eventually have to win over.
And indignation won't help. I at least tried to heed my own
advice.

Several hours and two dozen endorsements later, work had
pretty much tapered off. I was sitting on the floor listening
while Hawk, who was perched on the windowsill, instructed
his underling about parties and sex at antiwar conferences. He
parted with his knowledge on the subject between long, libidi-
nous drags on his Pall Mall. In the outer room Peter, Dick and
Sam were playing a quick game of baseball with a crumpled-up
piece of paper. I looked at my watch—it was eleven o'clock—
and started to get up.

"Well," I said, "I don't want to wake anyone up."

"Don't worry about it," Dave replied, returning to his file cards. "It's only eight o'clock in California. And I've got some names of good people to call in Hawaii."

I settled back down to the floor with a yawn.

"Well, maybe it *is* getting late," he said with a touch of irritation. "I suppose I should be getting back to some work at the NSA office anyway."

I couldn't believe it. Maybe sleeping was against his religion. But then I looked into the outer room where the baseball game had stopped and saw that Sam was on his way out the door for a late-night meeting with someone. Perhaps, I thought to myself, it's just some kind of Darwinian natural selection that puts non-sleeping mutants into antiwar organizing. I packed up my three-by-five cards and contact lists and put them neatly into the only available business file—between two rungs of a radiator. A minute later we were all out the door, down the elevator, and pushing through the double set of glass doors out onto the sidewalk.

Hawk puttered down Vermont Avenue on his Honda toward the NSA office, Dick went off to find his illegally parked Volvo, and Peter and I started toward Connecticut Avenue for a leisurely walk home. The stifling, humid air had cooled off to a mere eighty-five degrees, the sky was clear, and God—playful deity that he is—had the moon hanging out. It was 11:20, but there were still a fair number of cars passing silently below the buildings that were speckled with burning office lights. I guess even the prowar organizers go 'round the clock.

As we turned onto Connecticut I peered into one of the cars paused at the stoplight. At the wheel was a young but haggard-looking executive leaning against the open window of his car. As he loosened his tie he didn't notice that the light had turned green. But there was no clamor of horns or profanities as one hears in New York or Chicago, only an ab-

breviated *beep* from the car directly behind him. The startled
man, realizing that it was his turn, led the chain of autos noise-
lessly through the empty intersection. Everything in Washington was quiet compared to other major cities. Not the quiet of
inaction, but a kind of deliberating quietude of preoccupation.
Everyone seemed to be preoccupied with his own work and
how it would be *his* job that would make all the difference.

We walked on for another block in silence. At the corner
ahead a black limousine with miniature foreign flags on the
hood turned onto Connecticut going the other way. I tried to
picture myself riding in the back seat, on my way to a late-
night meeting with Nixon. I'd walk into the oval office, give
Dick the finger, and leave.

"Think it'll all come to anything?" Peter asked.

The question roused me from my thoughts before I had
a chance to imagine the expression on Nixon's face.

"Of course it will. Couldn't you tell just from the people
you talked to tonight?"

"Well, I suppose." Then he added hesitatingly, "It's just
that a lot of people have been through this kind of thing before. A lot of protests, but it's still the same type of people
that have the power to keep the war going."

It was long after midnight when we got back to the run-
down house near Dupont Circle that my friends and I had
rented for the summer. Drenched from a cold shower, I lay
on one of the upstairs beds, feeling a pleasantness and restful-
ness that I had almost forgotten could exist. I lay still as the
cooling beads of water slowly disappeared, for the first time
realizing just how physically exhausted I was from the long
day. But just this one day's work had created a satisfaction and
emotional resurgence that I had long ago dismissed as myth.
My whole life had been that of a student, reading about the
real world where people work, and vote, and catch buses.
Academia was reading all about it. But this day *I* had been

catching the buses and talking to people, finding out how they felt, and beginning to work with them about what they and I could do about those feelings. With a telephone and a shared belief, I was linking arms with people all over the country.

As I was being pulled under by my sleep, all the thoughts of the day swirled and overlapped—Sam Brown; the weary government executive driving home; the southern yelp of "Raht on!"; Hawk leaving on his Honda to work on into the night; the heat; the coolness; the "Student Call" that I had already memorized—" . . . Death and destruction are unabated; bombs and fire continue to devastate South Vietnam . . . " By the time my roommates came in I was fast asleep.

Over the next couple of days I met the other Moratorium organizers and found my own niche in the office setup. Dick and I began the work of making the initial conacts on the campuses. Hawk and Brown worked in the office to one side of us. In the office to the other side of us were the two other senior members of the Committee, Marge Sklencar and David Mixner.

Marge was an affable twenty-four-year-old with a girlish smile and laugh. If one thing held the Washington office together it was Marge. She was a veteran of the McCarthy and Lowenstein campaigns and during the off season was a grade school teacher. In later months national news media described her as everything from the "effeciency expert" to the "mother hen" of the staff. After sixteen-hour days of organizing non-campus communities and administrating our office, Marge always seemed to have a few more minutes to listen to all the personal problems besetting our extrapolitical lives. Beginning the day that Marge and I discovered we had both been raised in Milwaukee, we plagued the rest of the office with our little regional idioms. It was a full week before the rest of the disgruntled staff discovered that the "bubbler" Marge and I talked about was the drinking fountain in the hallway. One time I asked her to adopt me, but she only laughed.

If there was one member of the Committee that represented the Establishment end of the antiwar spectrum, it was David Mixner. This tall and hefty twenty-five-year-old had been a key organizer for all the non-primary states in the McCarthy campaign. I never really got to know David very well, since neither of us directed much conversation to the other: even if there had been reason to (and there wasn't, since we were organizing totally different segments of society), it would have been difficult, since Mixner's daily routine during the summer consisted of coming into the office for messages and then disappearing into the bowels of Capitol Hill for a day or two, where he lobbied for the Moratorium cause. His area of responsibility certainly made him the best dressed of the Committee. The people in Congress were the people Mixner knew best—they were also the ones in whom he put his trust. Political change for David seemed to be essentially electoral change. When I think back on it, I'm still amazed that the Committee was able to stay intact as long as it did—in one room Mixner was on the phone talking to congressmen about antiwar resolutions, while in another room Hawk was engaged in conversations about "power to the people" and militant resistance. That there was this type of diversity (or perhaps disparity) in the leadership is reflective of the kind of coalition that the Moratorium Committee was attempting to assemble. It wasn't until I returned to Cambridge in the fall that I realized this type of bedfellowship was doomed.

At this time Brown spent most of his time continuing to raise the badly needed funds to run the office.

"Nickels and dimes! That's all they're giving," he said one day, throwing down a return letter and small contribution (a couple of hundred) from another of the large McCarthy contributors. It was one of the rare times Sam openly showed his disgust. "And look at *this*." Sam reached into his desk drawer and handed me a letter of apology that had come a few days earlier. It was an explanation from one of the largest McCarthy contributors, and certainly one of the wealthiest men in the country, why he "wouldn't be able to help at this time."

Sam laughed with a touch of cynicism. "Even *he* knows that won't be the end of it." Only on certain occasions does Brown lose his deceiving appearance of boyish innocence— collection time is one such occasion. He turned back to the typewriter to compose a reply, a bit stiffer than the first solicitation, and as Sam predicted, its recipient didn't really intend to hold back all. The couple of thousand came a week later.

Aside from overseeing the work that Dick and I were doing with the campuses, Hawk's main responsibilities lay with coordinating the work of the Moratorium Committee with that of other antiwar groups. Because most other peace groups were a healthy quantum-level to the left of the Moratorium Committee and because Hawk was clearly the most radical of our group, he was a perfect liaison. In addition to that consideration, Hawk was also on the steering committee of the New Mobilization Committee, the large umbrella organization that was planning November protests in Washington, that connection placing him in an even more perfect position to do inter-organizational coordinating. As far as resident quasi-radicals go, Hawk was ideal.

Some time during the second or third day of obtaining the endorsements that would be unveiled at Sam's press conference and getting the organizations going on the campuses, Dick and I realized that the only logical way to distribute the work would be by regions. Thus we made our first critical policy decision independent of the rest of the antiwar movement—we got a map. Our next momentous decision, this one

requiring at least an hour of discussion, concerned the colors
of pins we would use to denote campus, state, and regional
coordinators. Once that was settled nothing stood between us
and our work except the choice of who would handle which
region. We sat in our swivel chairs, hands folded across our
laps, staring at our expansive and colorful wall map.

"Well," Dick began, "Sam says we'll probably be doing
a lot of traveling to check up on the campuses and everything."

"Do you feel like we're sitting in some kind of war room?"
I asked.

"Hmm" was the most acknowledgment Dick cared to
grant my statement. "I was saying that we'll probably be doing
a fair amount of traveling, so maybe we should think about
that in dividing up the country."

"You're right. My parents live in Wisconsin, and I have a
sister in California—I guess maybe I should take the western
half."

"That's just fine with me," Dick said. "Any friends I'd
want to stop and see while I'm organizing live in the East."

The decision consummated, history moved on. I took
everything from Ohio to Hawaii. He took the east.

Over the next two weeks the phone became another ap-
pendage to my body—day, night, weekends we raced to collect
as many college endorsements as possible. Since this part of
the movement was geared essentially to press relations, the
matter at times became a bit contrived. "Remember, the best
thing is to get as broad a set of endorsements as possible," one
of my fellow organizers remarked. That meant getting approval
from student leaders from every type of college this country
had to offer. The Berkeleys and Columbias alone wouldn't do.
We needed a couple of southern state schools, a few from the
Big Ten, one or two black colleges in the South. Notre Dame

would look good; so would Howard and Yeshiva. As a matter of fact, my last call to an eastern school before retreating to my own region went to the home of one of the student leaders at Yeshiva in New York.

"Hallo? Who's dis?" It was his father.

"Hello, is Danny there?"

"No, Dannila's not here. Dis a friend?"

"My name is Ken Hurwitz. I'm calling for the Vietnam Moratorium Committee."

"Dat's nice, but Dannila's got a 2S, zo I'll tell him you called."

"No, you don't understand," I said. "We're a group organizing a protest against the war. We'd like your son to help." New York politics and Jewish tradition told me I hadn't overstepped my introduction.

He turned to whoever was responsible for the blaring radio in the background. "Vill you turn dat down completely already!" Then he got back to me. "Dat's nice, but it's Saturday morning—Dannila's at shul. I'm sick, so I'm here." An extremely convincing cough followed. "A nice Jewish name like Hurvitch and you daunt know my son's gonna be at shul?"

"I'm sorry, I forgot." Raised in an upper-middle-class suburb, a nice Jewish kid can forget a lot of things. "Tell Danny I'll call again, will you?"

"Yeah, sure, I'll tell him. Be a good boy."

I hung up and tried to be.

The calling went on. As the days passed I began to notice a growing flexibility in my own approach to the task of organizing, a flexibility that was necessary for all the organizers if the wide coalition that the Moratorium sought was to ever materialize. Depending upon the political bent of my listener, I would emphasize different aspects of the war, just as long as the same conclusion would emerge in every case—that the war had to be ended by a complete and immediate American withdrawal. I felt rather uncomfortable at times, dwelling with some on what I believed to be the selfish and myopic reasoning for wanting out, rather than always addressing myself directly to the more basic issue involved, namely America's aggression. Certainly many people, I felt, had all the wrong reasons for being against the war—"The war's unwinnable," "It's hurting our economy," et cetera. But the special immediacy of ending a war that was taking several thousand lives each week somehow made all the varying reasons irrelevant. The only critical question really was whether or not someone was willing to join the demand for immediate withdrawal.

To be sure, there were always pressures from both sides to expand the breadth of dialogue. From the left always came the pressure to talk about the war in terms of capitalism versus communism and America's role all around the world, to have socialist speakers at the Moratorium rallies, not to ally with "liberal politicians," and so forth. And on the "right" were people like Allard Lowenstein (Dem. N.Y.) who until the fall had refused to support the Moratorium because its platform didn't include a condemnation of campus radicals. On the narrow line between, attempting to keep the dialogue centered on the points to which everyone who was antiwar would agree, walked, sometimes tiptoed, the Moratorium Committee.

By June 30 we hadn't quite attained the goal of one hundred endorsements—we had ninety-six, to be exact, but that was close enough for the reporters covering the press conference to use the one hundred figure. My role at the conference was strictly one of a spectator, and the piled-up work at the office nearly kept me from even that.

I got to the Hilton an hour after it had begun, and the green-carpeted room was already stale with smoke. Almost all the pastry ordered for the guests had been snatched and gobbled between questions, and only a cup or two of coffee remained in the large silver server at the rear of the room. I helped myself to a cup of coffee and dropped down into the smothering comfort of a Hilton chair. Only over time did I come to recognize many of these reporters' faces—they came from the *New York Times*, the *Washington Post*, the *Boston Globe*, the *New York Post*, and the AP wire service. Sam was just about wrapping things up, answering questions from some of the still-skeptical reporters.

"Mr. Brown," came a voice from this sea of backs of heads, "what would you consider an acceptable troop level in Vietnam, I mean for you to discontinue the protests?"

"No troops at all," was Brown's answer as he put down his own cup of coffee. "In Korea today we still have about sixty-five thousand troops." He stepped forward as if to attack with the pen he was holding. "A Korean-type settlement for Vietnam is totally unacceptable."

"Do you think the adult community is going to be very impressed by more campus protests?" The question came from the cigar region of the room, its tone as pungent as the smoke that accompanied it.

"I think in October parents are going to realize that it's not only the two or three percent 'radicals' but more like seventy percent that are protesting—'their sons and daughters.'" As it turned out it was the two or three percent "radicals" who would be *against* the Moratorium.

Then came a pause—Brown surveyed the room, but there were no more takers. With the shifting in chairs and rustling of closing notebooks it was clear that the Moratorium Committee's first press conference was over. As the members of the press filed out—some in their late twenties, some considerably older—Brown shook hands with many and thanked them individually for coming. The antiwar fervor was gone from his voice—a sprinkling of that boyish diffidence had returned. It seemed that no matter what the occasion was, whether it was dealing with the press or congressmen or his own Moratorium staff, Sam had a way of making others feel that they had just done him a great favor. And when you have that feeling, especially after having done nothing, it becomes extremely difficult to refuse any request that may follow.

Some, pausing to talk with him, reminisced about the colder, snowblown days in New Hampshire with the McCarthy entourage. Reminiscing seems to be one of the genuinely visceral enjoyments of political activists and the press men who follow them. Whether it's the civil rights days in Mississippi or the itinerant months of '68, there's always time to analogize between past and present politics and see the latter as the logical extension of the former. It's all connected, the people, the times, the places. New faces are added as the old ones cross paths year after year in this new project or that new campaign. Sam Brown's was a face in transition—not totally new, but certainly not old, still moving from one to the other. By the end of the year that transition was complete.

By early July, I had for the most part acclimated myself to a new lifestyle in Washington, D.C. We had by this time left that first abortion of a house and moved into a three-bedroom, spectacularly air-conditioned home on Twenty-fifth Street.

There was even a place around the corner to put Nader —that was the 1963 Corvair that Bob and I had purchased at the beginning of the summer for $250. The last week of August a car mechanic offered us $15—$18 if we'd put in three bucks' worth of gas. We eventually sold the car for a bit more, but I hated to part with it—so many fine memories. Like the day it stalled forty-three times going through the Delaware Bridge toll gate in heavy traffic, or the night it learned to smoke on the Wisconsin Avenue hill.

After more than two weeks in the city we had all become despicably routinized. I was working at the Moratorium office

until evening, making myself dinner at about eight o'clock—
six out of seven nights that meant my famous bacon cheeseburger, the seventh it was a cheese-covered baconburger. After
dinner I'd try to write a little—an obnoxious play that my roommate, Peter, co-authored and which we humanely put to sleep
in August. Another of my roommates, Mark, spent most of
June and July looking for a job. By the end of July he only
looked at the clock, waiting for August when he could leave
and visit his brother in Arizona. Bob, on the other hand, was
really in the thick of it. He followed police cars for the *Washington Post* from six in the evening until three in the morning,
a job for only their top analysts.

Most disturbing of all was the empty mailbox that rattled
every day outside my front door. Sometimes when I was alone
I even peeked out through the curtain when the mailman was
coming up the walk, but no, he wasn't pocketing any letters
from Marcie. She just wasn't writing, and I was nearly cracking. Finally, after close to a month, a few letters began dribbling
in from Europe, and as I had suspected, it was all about that
independence thing again. Not ready to settle down, must be
free and mentally unmarried, too young for total commitment,
and painful *et ceteras*. Every morning I trudged into the office
with more tales of woe.

"I'm going nuts with this thing," I moaned to Dick. "Has
this ever happened to *you?*"

"Has it ever happened to *me!*" he ridiculed my question.
"Do bears shit in the woods? Of course it's happened to me.
Just have a little cool, and wait until she gets back. Things
will be just fine, no need to get an ulcer."

With only limited success I tried to heed the advice.

Peter, on the other hand, seemed to be very happy with
everything about his summer life. The research in Ribicoff's
office was appealing, and the Senate intern baseball games in

the evenings were inspiring. Sometimes even the senators themselves would consent to play an inning or two.

Coming home one night at about nine o'clock, I found Peter at the zenith of his political and baseball career. He was curled up on the couch, clutching his baseball mitt. This had been the day Ribicoff's office had played McCarthy's crew. But the big thrill was that Clean Gene himself had decided to play. And if that weren't enough to make Peter's July complete, the last play of the game was a fly ball off the wood of big Gene's bat that was caught in a phenomenal leap by— guess who—"Say hey" Peter Shulman! The last hopes of the McCarthy office team were dashed to the ground (or rather caught in the mitt) of *my* roommate! As the weary soldiers headed for the showers (to be followed by the usual hours in the Washington bars) the big gray-haired man himself slapped Peter on the shoulder and told him it was a "great catch," a quote I was to hear several thousand times over the next two months. And I missed it all, all except the sight of the drunken star whimpering with joy into his never-the-same-again mitt.

The work with the Moratorium was steadily more encouraging, though still undramatic. A mass mailing of over thirty-five hundred pieces had been sent out to every college student-body president and newspaper editor in the country. Almost all the replies were favorable. No more than once every few weeks would we get a "you've turned your back on Christ" letter in return. The press conference had made newsprint in all the desirable columns, but only in the eastern papers, and thus I still needed to explain to many of "my western people" on the phone who and what the Moratorium was.

I was getting to know (at least, as well as one gets to know anything over the phone) the new and old voices of the antiwar movement. The new ones were mainly the students, many, like myself, for the first time putting actions behind their dinner-table beliefs. In each of us was that intriguing blend of optimism and skepticism—not enough experience to stick with either for very long. Most of the old ones were the professors, the ones who had seen one idea to end the war after another fade into the history of the '60s. But now all were agreed on one thing. We had been silent for too long. Now was the time to begin again. Once in October, twice in November, and again and again, nonviolent dialogue with our neighbors for as long as it would take. They felt the strategy was right. At least in academia, that large moderate left was being moved.

Late in the summer a phone expert confirmed our suspicions that our phones were being tapped. There lay a sad farce. We were hardly a clandestine group that planned anything in the office that wasn't told in detail to the press. But obviously the government didn't bother itself over that sort of detail. The point, then, is how the men who run this country view protest, that *any* protest, even as moderate and overt as the Moratorium, will be surreptitiously investigated. And that point *was* something to be considered.

After two summers of work in a surgery department had changed my ideas about being the great healer, I had envisioned my "contribution to the world" as coming through a career in government. But now I was discovering exactly what government was all about. Just by being part of this office and being listened to by wiretappers, I was clearly developing my own little FBI file. I had already, I'm sure, precluded certain future security clearances. But then, was the government something that I really wanted? The pragmatic advice I always hear is to rock the boat a little, but not enough to hurt my future— wait until I'm in a position of power where my dissent will mean much more. The only fallacy with the argument, of course, is that that position never arrives. There's another place even grander in the hierarchy than the last one, always another day when I'll be even more "influential." It wasn't a waiting game I cared to play. If joining an antiwar group meant closing off certain career avenues, then I'd rather recognize the dead-end of those careers now than a sorrowfully co-opted forty years from now. Of course, by the fall the Moratorium had become totally Establishmentized, with endorsements from everyone from Averell Harriman to Cardinal Cushing, hardly giving me that "banished from government" feeling. But in early summer when it looked as though it might be only the young pro-testers on one side and the government on the other, I for-tunately had a different perspective on what this might do or not do to my future—fortunate in that I was forced to give thought to what I would or would not be willing to give up to join that government, that "rest of society." Only as alterna-tives are removed do we know where we draw the line.

CHAPTER TWO

Death's a bummer.
—ANONYMOUS TEENY-BOPPER

Finding a slogan for the Moratorium proved to be easy: "October 15—Work for Peace." But choosing a graphic design to embellish the leaflets, flyers, and buttons was quite another story. The debate over that detail of our campaign was concluded on Saturday morning near the end of July when the people from the advertising agency came to town.

"Oh, yes," I had said emotionlessly when handed the design for the button. "But what's the significance of the porpoise?"

"That's not a porpoise, that's a dove!" Connie, the artist, replied stiffly.

"Oh yes," I said for a second time. "But why is it throwing up?"

That was the cue for the chief sugar-daddy of the advertising outfit (hereafter referred to as Peace Pusher). From across the room he gave me a wink and smile, the kind that nearly connects the winking eye with the raised lip along that side of the face, and clicked his tongue like the sound of a cocking trigger.

"All cuteness aside," he said, "I'm sure you see that's an olive branch hanging from its mouth." He swaggered over to me and pointed at the sample print on my lap. "There—right there—don't you see the leaves there?" He pointed at the lumpy vomit that was dripping from the porpoise's mouth. At this point the artist and the two other ad men joined in huddling over me as though they were waiting for a doctor's final verdict of an X ray. Not wanting to disappoint them, I looked up and said solemnly, "It's malignant." Like most of my jokes, it elicited laughs from Brown, Marge, and Dick, and plaintive sighs from the others. Mixner, our congressional organizer, was beginning to chew on his ring.

"Trust me on this," Peace Pusher continued. "I've done PR for a hell of a lot of antiwar projects. Peace is my game, and I'm telling you"—he paused and put his hand on my shoulder—"really quite frankly now, this dove is going to *make* the Moratorium." His hand still rested on my shoulder, gently trying to massage me into his camp. An extended debate over the dove ensued.

"No offense to Ken," Hawk interjected wearily after some time, "But the minority has to be overruled. Let's not make this a Quaker meeting that drags on all morning."

"I don't want to be here all day, either," Brown said, "but I'd prefer if we could all agree on the design." There were still only a half-dozen of us in the Moratorium Committee at this time, and Brown, being the head, wanted as much office unity as possible. It was just his style to hear everyone out, including Dick and me, the "junior members" of the Committee. In Social Relations 120, my encounter-group course at school, Sam would have been ordained "maintenance leader."

Brown came over and looked intently at the bird on my lap. "I think maybe the reason it looks a bit aquatic," he said, "is because of the neck. It's kind of a hump where it should go down. Here, give me that for a second." He took the sketch pen and began zestfully revamping while Connie calmly put her finger in her mouth and puffed up her cheeks as though she were going to blow herself up. After a minute or two with his carbon-tipped butcher knife, Sam stepped back. Sam Brown's a great organizer, but a van Gogh he's not. The bird now looked like a white bowling ball.

"Now *that's* a dove!" I exclaimed.

Peace Pusher, knowing that Brown was the one who ran our group, nodded appreciatively at the abomination Sam had just produced. "Yes, well . . . uh . . ." He was having difficulty maintaining his pin-striped smile. "We'll work on it for a couple of days and show you what we come up with." Connie was already packing up her samples.

"Yeah, I think we like the basic idea," Sam said. I felt I had already taken up enough time with my obstinacy (and would have been outvoted anyway), so I added my gutteral agreement to the chorus. We all stood up and moved toward the door. Everyone shook hands, though mine didn't get too much of a workout. The peacenik entrepreneurs left, and I returned to my desk for more calling. Marge had sent out for sandwiches for all of us. Gratefully I accepted a cheeseburger, but my mouth was just watering for roasted dove.

A few days later Hawk poked his head through the door to Dick and my office and asked us if we wanted to accompany him on a "business-pleasure trip" to the Atlantic City Pop Festival. It seemed like a great idea. For the first six weeks of the summer we had been organizing the Moratorium by phone out of our office in Washington. Six uninterrupted weeks of "dial-a-movement." Day after day, just me and that green plastic thing on my desk—the "shit work" of political organizing. When Hawk waved the tickets to the rock festival in front of me, my eyes assumed the glazed look of delirium of a bedridden patient about to be turned over. What could provide a better break in routine than distributing our literature and talking to people about the Moratorium in between listening to the rock groups that were warming up for Woodstock? That whole week I looked forward to the following Friday morning when we would be leaving for three days of good sounds and facile political organizing. No hard-nosed persuading necessary —we would be among the peaceniks, "our people."

But car trips never seem to leave when they're supposed to; ours to Atlantic City was no exception. The morning, then part of the afternoon passed as one delay after another had us scurrying around Washington. First wrestling Dick Lavine's Volvo back from the car mechanic, then getting a hurried and harassed printer to finish the thousands of leaflets and information packets that were to be distributed at the Pop Festival, then this, then that. By the time we got on the road it was late afternoon. Dick, his girlfriend, Marti, and I were in one car, Dave and an old girlfriend of his in another. Few of the girls drifting in and out of the office seemed to be able to resist Dave Hawk, bon vivant of the antiwar movement. Not that this interfered with Hawk's long and hard hours of work—it's just that violence and sex are but two sides of the same mattress (or battlefield, if you prefer) and that they occupy the human life in inverse proportion. Anyone who organizes against one is certain to salute the other.

By the time we got to Atlantic City it was eleven o'clock, pouring rain, and the first night of performances had just ended. As we passed the racetrack and adjoining stands where the festival was being held, we could see the shadowy and silhouetted fans running about trying to set up their tents for the night before they were washed into the ocean. Some who didn't have tents were standing in the rain-slicked road trying to hitch a ride to shelter—some were just standing on the grass with their faces tilted toward the clouds, enjoying the warm summer splash of the water and the inevitability of their predicament. But since we hadn't brought any camping equipment and the "sky as our blanket" bit had been ruled out, we decided to get a motel room for the night. The only way to convey that message to Hawk and his friend, however, was to call Marge in Washington to tell her where we were staying and then hope that Hawk would also check in with her. Well, somehow it all worked out and the five of us spent the night in a motel single about five miles from the racetrack. It was all very cozy, no one minding that everyone else walked around the room nude. I convinced myself that I wasn't a fifth wheel but that they were all superfluous additions to a unicycle. I went to sleep amid the orchestrated snores, looking forward to a weekend of rock music and some face-to-face political rapping without the separation of Bell Telephone's long-distance static.

The next day was Saturday morning, a spectacularly sunny morning. After a great and greasy lunch that only my generation could appreciate we piled into the cars and headed for the racetrack. The first two miles were fine, but then we hit the caravan. Thousands of cars were bumper to bumper, moving from slow to slower. One fellow in the back of a station wagon reached out the open rear window and tagged the hood of the car behind, calling, "You're it!" The racetrack parking lot had long been filled up, and now cars were just trying to find some room along the roadside. We would have done exactly that except for the reams upon reams of literature we had to carry into the stands for distribution. As traffic came to a near standstill Marti and I hopped out of the car with bundles of Moratorium flyers in our arms, and carried them from car to car. Every now and then things began moving again and we just stood in the middle of the two lanes handing the sheets to the cars as they came past at about three or four miles an hour. Sometimes an iridescently painted VW bus would come past, all loaded down with a weekend's worth of food and drink. In return for the leaflets I gratefully accepted an ice cube here, a piece of watermelon there. One likeable fellow tossed me a joint, which I put in my shirt pocket for the night back at the motel.

The business continued this way for another mile or so— sometimes my standing still, handing out the flyers to the air-polluting conveyor belts that passed on either side of me, sometimes their standing still waiting for this disheveled pedestrian to come to them. When I had finished giving out my bundle, I looked around for Dick's car, but it was nowhere in sight, nor was Marti. I then proceeded to look for a car with all girls. When one would come along I would clutch my throat with one hand and stick out the thumb of my other. The first two passed me by (damn teeny-boppers!), but the third picked me up (mature women!). I rode the rest of the way being pitied with pretty smiles and lemonade.

Once at the racetrack we all met in front of the main stadium entrance, where we set up our literature depot, a place we could return to for resupplying and meeting after the last performances that night. Gathering up armfuls of the flyers and info sheets, we wished each other good vibrations and went to mingle with as many as possible of the 90,000 that showed up for the weekend. Barely managing to get one free finger out to show my ticket at the gate, I entered the dark concrete labyrinth beneath the stands. Echoing off the walls was the high-pitched harmony of the Byrds, singing a one-time hit that was now a "golden-oldie memory maker, gone from the charts but not from our hearts." I began walking to the beat of the music until I came, like Dante, to the abrupt light and open air of the other side (well, not *exactly* like Dante, but reasonably close). Once in the open air, I could hear much more distinctly the words of the song. "To everything, turn, turn, turn;

there is a season, turn, turn, turn." The words were from Ecclesiastes, the tune from Pete Seeger. Neither had been invited to the festival.

Looking up and to my back, I could see the row upon row of brightly dressed people extending up to the flat metallic stadium roof. Passing out the literature up there would be easy, but talking to anyone other than those on the aisle seats would be nearly impossible, so I decided to just wander around on the slanted slab of concrete that lay between the seats and the track. During the horseracing season, this is where the small-time betters stand—between their feet and the concrete is the bed of losers' unclaimed betting tickets. But for this weekend the grounds-keepers had swept away the losing ticket stubs— swept the place clean for the new inhabitants. Slowly I picked my way through the standing, sitting, and lying groups of people. Some were listening intently to the band on the stage —now it was the Creedence Clearwater Revival—some were sitting in small groups, talking or passing a joint or both, some were just stretched out trying to catch a few rays in between the intruding shadows such as my own. Many were dressed like me, in jeans and a T-shirt, but most were a good deal more hip, wearing bell-bottoms, ruffled shirts, "granny" sunglasses, and, oh yes, bands. There were arm bands, leg bands, head bands, finger bands (sometimes called rings), neck bands, ankle bands—it was a sea of bands. Most were colorfully and skill-fully hand-fashioned, though one I saw was just a modified jock strap.

Just as quickly as I could I began handing out the flyers and pamphlets to everyone within reach. I tried to skip no one. I leafleted the sunbathers, the fence leaners, the girls perched atop their boyfriends' shoulders, the people trying to get a better view from the tops of the sound trucks, everyone. I even climbed up a ladder in order to put a couple of them in

the hands of a guy and his girlfriend who were sitting literally
inside one of the giant speakers that was in front of the stage.
Huddled on a ledge of this mammoth amplifier's metal grid,
the two of them, reverberating with each twang of a guitar and
beat of a drum, never opened their eyes. They only closed
their hands around the paper I put against their palms, and
continued nodding with the music. I doubted whether they
could still hear it.

But from all the standing, sitting, and stretched-out people
I gave our information packets to, the reaction was nearly always
the same. A few read what I gave them, but most only glanced
at the first page and tossed it aside. Most of those who *did* make
it to the last page stopped there. It was on that page we in-
cluded a mail-in form for name and address so we could send
the person more information about how to organize the Moratorium in his home community. They would nod at the first
couple of pages, mumble some kind of approbation, and then,
when reaching that last page, let the pamphlet drop incon-
spicuously from their hands. I was beginning to get annoyed.

Once siphoned of my material, I went back to our depot
for new supplies, but this time waited until the bands took one
of their periodic fifteen-minute breaks before continuing. Since
everyone (including myself) wanted to listen to the music, it
seemed I would have more success if I waited for a break when
I could get into conversations with the people about the
autumn and protest-organizing.

In another half hour the music stopped. As people passed
me on their way for food or just a walk, I again began handing
out my wares and talking "carnie" style about the coming
October 15. Everyone accepted a leaflet, but no one stopped to
talk. Every now and then I twisted my head to see the reaction
of those who had passed and now had the sheets in their hands.
But most weren't in their hands anymore—almost all of them

were on the ground. The place where the losing betting stubs used to be was now fertilized with the words "October 15th— Work for Peace."

About an hour later I found the first person who wanted to talk. He was a fellow with shoulder-length curly brown hair and a peace medallion around his neck.

"Hey man, whach ya got there?" he asked. I handed him a packet and began explaining what the Moratorium was all about.

"Oh, dig it, man! Like peace is really a heavy thing." He bounced on his toes as he spoke. "You know, like it's really somethin' I can get my head into and relate to. Wow, like a Moratorium for peace—far fuckin' out!"

Ecstatic that I was finally getting something more than sympathetic apathy, I told him to be sure to return the tear-off sheet so we could stay in touch about organizing the Moratorium in his home town or campus.

"Oh no, man," he said at that. "Like the whole peace thing's a real groove, but politics just isn't where my head's at right now." Then he gave me the sheets back, thanked me, and left.

And that's just about how things went for the rest of the day and night. One girl held up her hand waving off my attempt to give her a flyer, telling me that she "just didn't want to think about the war." It wasn't, of course, hostility that I was receiving, the kind I might have gotten in conservative suburbs or farmlands. On the contrary, my cause got only sympathy, but useless sympathy. Everyone there thought that peace was just great, but that "politics" was too depressing. I was quickly learning that antiwar sentiment doesn't necessarily equal political activism. Politics happened to be my thing—it didn't happen to be theirs. The rest of that day and night I continued learning.

Once in a while I would meet up with Dick and Marti or

Hawk and his girl—they seemed to be having about the same degree of success. We agreed to meet back at our makeshift depot when the show was over.

After handing out my last piece of literature around ten-thirty, I spent the last half hour of the show sprawled on the infield of the track, listening to the Jefferson Airplane. Gracie Slick was really tearing the crowd up. "Some pills make you larger, some pills make you small. But the pills that Mother gives you, they don't do anything at all." I lay still on the slightly damp grass, looking straight into the speckled, black sky. The electricity of the music was all around me—in the air above me, on my sides, even shaking the soft ground below me. I tried to think, but I couldn't. The music was too demanding. It was emotionally taut, sensual, at times destructive. It vibrated in my ears and in every part of my body. I lay on my back and every now and then I could see from the feet up the elongated figure of someone half walking, half dancing past me. I tried to concentrate, but it was impossible. Every blade of grass seemed to quiver as the drums and electric guitars blasted from the mammoth speakers. Gracie Slick with sweat running down her cheeks was really wailing. "When logic and good fortune have given you the call, and the White Knight is talking backward. . . . " I could feel the bass guitar throbbing in the pit of my stomach, I could only feel. I lay on the grass, my arms and legs extended. My fingers were burrowing into the moist earth. The music never relented. It echoed and re-echoed off the metal and the concrete and the people. It penetrated every part of everything that was present, and I just stopped trying to think.

The next day, Sunday, was like the day before it, beautifully sunny, maybe even a little *too* hot. Since the afternoon show didn't start until one-thirty, we decided to drive the few miles into Atlantic City and take in a little surf and sun. It was my first time in Atlantic City. For those of you who don't know this weighty fact, Atlantic City happens to be the place upon which Parker Brothers modelled their game Monopoly. What a surprise it was driving past street signs like "Ventnor," "Marvin Gardens," and "Park Place!" Disappointed, though, that none of these streets had little green houses or big red hotels on them, we went directly to the beach. And there it was, the elusive goal of my entire childhood, the treasure that my brother and sister always secured on those long, rainy afternoons but which always seemed to evade my sweaty grasp, the prize of every red-blooded ten-year-old capitalist—Boardwalk!!! It turned out to be a half-mile-long warped splinter-factory with a few sunburned hot-dog vendors.

After changing into our swim suits (I was in my polka-dotted queenie drawers), we spread our collective flesh across the sand. What strange pleasure the Caucasian race takes in this practice of partial self-immolation—giving the body a trial by fire. And when we had destroyed enough of our skin cells to please, it was time to join the rest of the tanned lemmings in a little body surfing. Have you ever body surfed on a Sunday at the Atlantic City Boardwalk? Have you ever tried to play chess at five o'clock on a New York subway? Both can be done, and both are the pastimes of masochists. Once I accepted the notion, however, of riding the wave in on someone else's body, I actually became quite proficient. And it was a good way to meet people as well, although the introduction was never complete until the wave had deposited us all on the beach.

After two such joy rides, we transported our reddened carcasses back to the racetrack. This day, matters improved musically (Janis Joplin, Little Richard, and other soul-on-the-sleeve wailers), but politically it was an even rounder zero than the day before. Clearly, this just wasn't the place to get commitments to help organize for the fall protests. From the thousands of leaflets that we distributed, we received maybe sixty replies through the mail.

That night after the show was over I was more than happy to get into Dick's cramped Volvo and head back to Washington. As the car ground south along the highway, gradually leaving behind the rest of the traffic and lights, I sat in the welcome darkness of the back seat, pondering my confusion, my disappointment—yes, even, at times, my anger. I had been to rock concerts before, millions of them, but I had never gone as a politico. This time I looked twice at the "cultural revolution" that I had been told I was part of.

Sometimes I see people wearing buttons saying "peace and music" or buttons with the peace symbol along with an inscription such as "spirit of Woodstock." The assumption, I would suppose, is that the two worlds (the antiwar movement and the rock culture) are one in the same. Wrong. Granted there are connections—that the average antiwar worker is more likely to smoke grass than drink, dress hip than straight, be young than old, listen to the Rolling Stones than Mantovani. But from these connections (often the most superficial), to plunge ahead and force the rest of the analogy is a mistake. It is to mistake the visible, physical level for the whole. Jerry Rubin or Abbie Hoffman, the Chicago Conspiracy defendants, would argue that indeed the full analogy between the two worlds can be made, that it is necessary to create revolution within oneself before attempting to create one in the world, that drugs and music are the internal counterparts to political action. I can agree only in part. It is true that the antiwar movement and the rock culture share a certain general sense of humanitarianism, but there is a crucial difference in the direction of this instinct. In the activist it is externally oriented, in the rock culturalist it is totally internalized, withdrawn, and at times hedonistic.

The average fan at Atlantic City was one who would wear a peace button, talk (and not necessarily insincerely) about peace and tolerance, and, yes, some even attend protest demonstrations as religiously as the Manhattan wealthy attend the theater. But for most of these people all these actions are very personalized, in a sense existential. It is a part of "doing one's thing." It is a personal decision, not an effort to organize or influence others. This is perhaps the difference between the rock culturalist and the activist. The latter admittedly must be arrogant and self-assured enough to believe that he does know what's right for those around him—otherwise he wouldn't spend his time organizing. I felt anger for the former, the archetypal rock fan who takes his music and drugs not just as a particular form of entertainment, but as a way of life, a totally inner-directed life, because it seemed he was doing no more than the businessman who "looks the other way."

This isn't to say that everyone must be an organizer. I'm not *that* self-righteous. But it is to say that the belief that an *entire* life can be divorced from the greater world, that one need never do anything more than "his own thing" is only an updated, slightly hipper version of the John Stuart Mill myth that one can, if he wants, completely withdraw and thereby never adversely affect a fellow human being. But of course we *do* affect other human beings all the time, even if only by our tacit approval of the status quo. In fact, the prerequisite affluence and opportunities in this country for "doing our own things" are often derived from and founded upon the exploitation and sufferings of others. Whether we like it or not we are part of a nation that is involved in oppressing people at home and abroad. To believe we can lead our personal lives without being a part of that oppression is conscience-salving illusion. And to a large extent much of what falls under the banner of "cultural revolution" is exactly that. It is a recognition of what is wrong (and perhaps even of what should be done), but is at the same time a retreat from what that recognition would prescribe.

I stretched out on the back seat, my eyes fixed on the grungy ceiling of the car. I like to have room when I sulk.

"Can't this heap of shit ride any smoother?" I asked with a pleasant growl.

"We're parked in a station getting gas," Dick replied calmly, rather enjoying my bad mood. I propped my head up to view the embarrassing truth. "You're just sore," he added, "because the hippies have less use for you than you have for them."

"I'm not sore," I shouted, dropping my head back down to the sound of skull against ashtray.

For the next four hours my cynicism (gradually mellowing) and I rode somewhat uncomfortably on a back seat that seemed to shy away from the padded parts of my anatomy. By the time we reached Washington my body was indented and distended like any other Detroit-manufactured part. As we were reaching the outskirts of the city, I raised myself up to a sitting position and peered out between the mosquito corpses on the windshield. Dick's window was rolled down, and I let the cool damp air blow and lift the hair from my forehead. The sun was just beginning to pull its fat red belly over the horizon, and the traffic lights, their ambers blinking, had still another hour or two before being asked to control another day of regulated chaos.

The whole weekend in Atlantic City seemed more than a night's drive in the distance. The long ride had ameliorated, if not totally dissipated, my anger. In fact, despite the philosophical differences I had with the throngs at the racetrack, I was regretting now that I had placed myself at emotional odds with them. Some people I want to be against, people with whom I consider pridefully our mutual opposition—the George Wallaces and Barry Goldwaters, for example. But these weren't they. These people and I had so many like conclusions—just different ways of acting upon those conclusions.

We rounded the curve circumscribing Dupont Circle, the Haight-Ashbury of Washington, D.C., and I looked out at the dozens of people who were sitting listening to the music that a few of them were playing. Many had been up all night, as they were *every* night, with nothing to do. They just sat and listened. Most no longer believed in the possibility of political change or in the possibility of change or in the possibility. It seemed I would never feel like that, but perhaps some of them once told themselves the same thing. As we came to the end of the curve I smiled at the fellow playing the bongos and he smiled back. A nice time of day, dawn.

CHAPTER THREE

> *And He called the lightness day,*
> *and the darkness Texas.*
> —GENESIS

"El Paso?!"

"That's right," Sam said. It was early August and Sam had just arrived back from a trip to Europe.

"As in El Paso, Texas?" I asked, trying to make my voice squeakier to emphasize the incredulity.

"That's the one all right. University of Texas at El Paso. You better start packing."

"What's to pack? I'll take my fly swatter on the plane with me."

Sam continued rummaging through the molding stockpiles of phone messages on his desk. The Moratorium had begun its adolescent growth spurt, and Brown had dozens of people to get back to if the growth were to continue. "Sam, call Galbraith at home." "Goodwin called, will call again when you're back." "Brown, get in touch with McCarthy's office." No one ever left messages like that for me. I was impressed.

"Have you ever been to an NSA congress before?" he asked

as he swept his haul of used tea bags, straws, Coke bottles, and a month-old *New York Times* into a waiting get-away basket. "They're really great fun. You go to workshops, meet students from all around the country, politic all night at the plenaries. I went to a million of them." All the National Student Association reminded me of was the CIA. "Believe me, you'll love it. Marge is making the plane reservations for you and Hawk and Lavine right now."

Texas! Lyndon Johnson, H. L. Hunt, Lee Harvey Oswald, oil, the Dallas Cowboys, Fess Parker, and the Alamo. It's an obscene, objectively evil state, and I was determined to dislike it.

Paula, the receptionist and 'round-the-clock secretary, pushed her head through the door of the small office. "Sam, Walinsky's here."

"Great, tell him to come in." Sam straightened his tie so all the flowers on it could catch the full moonlight and brushed off his blue jeans. "Trader Vic's will have to take me as I am."

In walked the man. Definitely impressive. Brown suit, deep blue shirt, gold tie. The shine off his wing-tips nearly caused me retina damage.

"Good to see you, Adam," Sam said. "I'd like you to meet one of our campus coordinators, Ken Hurwitz. Ken, this is Adam Walinsky." He crushed my hand and shook the remains vigorously. When it was over I felt like calling it a day and going to bed. So this was the man, former legislative assistant to Bobby Kennedy, now running for Attorney General in New York, allegedly the quickest mind in Washington. "A pleasure to meet you, Mr. Walinsky." I kept my right hand behind my back where I could practice opening and closing it.

"Say, maybe Adam would like to see the map of campus coordinators," Sam suggested. "Sure," I said, "I'd be glad to show it to you." We moved to the door that separated Sam's office from Dick's and mine. They were entering *my* domain—

I would give the "casual host" role a whirl. Before either could object, I placed my hand on the edge of the door and drew it open, thus forming an archway with my arm under which they could pass. When you're tall this is a very smooth and appreciated gesture. When you're short, however, it's a total flight from reason. But it was too late, I was committed to my stance. They just had to enjoy crouching down as though they were entering a cave.

"So these are all the organizers," Walinsky said as he resurfaced on the other side.

"Yeah, that's them all right," I replied, embarrassed by the show and tell I had been placed in. Flashes of grammar school vaguely suggested that Brown was about to ask me to point out Arizona and name the capital. We stood there, the three of us, staring at a wall map of the United States, nodding.

"You've got hundreds of pins here," Walinsky finally said after tiring of nodding.

"Yep, hundreds," I agreed.

"Great organization here, just great." To add a little strength to the otherwise drab statement, Walinsky clenched his fist and rapped it solidly on Nova Scotia. *Plip*—first one pin —*plop, plip*, then three, then eight, then dozens of pins began falling from the map. "Oh, Jesus, I'm sorry," he stammered as more and more pins gave up the ghost and plunged to the linoleum below. Within another couple of seconds all but a few of my green campus, blue regional, and red state coordinators lay on the floor.

"My God," I gasped, "you just put the antiwar movement back to the end of June. All over the country Moratorium organizers are keeling over dead." Despite the attempted levity, Walinsky was feeling bad about his blunder. He began to pick up the pins and tried to find their rightful homes.

"No, really," I objected, "I'll get all of those later."

"Well, OK, if you insist, but, Jesus, I'm sorry about this."

"Really, I know where they all belong. It'll take me a minute." It took me two days.

"Well, all right. If you say so. Come on, Sam, we better be on our way to dinner." As they went through the outer door I called goodby to them from my hands and knees. Five minutes and six replaced pins later Marge wandered into my office.

"Here's your plane ticket and two hundred dollars—that should cover all your other expenses." When it came to office expenditures, Marge was always so serious and official-sounding, the grade-school teacher afraid her flippancy would lead to a neglect of the assignment.

"Not now, Marge." I continued on all fours, my nose five inches off the ground. "I'm looking for the guy who's organizing Utah."

"Yeah, well, when you're through, the stuff'll be on your desk."

Two nights later—at eleven o'clock on a Friday night, to be exact—Dick and I stood on a downtown corner of El Paso, Texas. It was a dry ninety degrees and absolutely silent. My worst visions of the city had been far inadequate. It was the ghostliest non-ghost town I had ever encountered, the largest unmarked grave in the country. We stood on the curb, halfway between the two hotels that were to house the thousand NSA representatives and student-body presidents (who were yet to arrive), our hands in our pockets, waiting. No cars, no people. The traffic lights changed for a third time, the clicking machinery inside the light changer sounding like thunder. Several blocks away I thought I perceived—could it be?—yes, headlights coming toward the intersection, and if he could only step on it, he would still have the green.

"Think he'll make it?" I asked Dick.

"A nickel says he doesn't have a chance." *Ach pooh* on big betters.

"Come on, baby," I coaxed what was now close enough to be seen as a '57 Chevy. "Give her the gas, A. J."

The car still a block away, the "don't walk" sign for that direction began flashing. Had there been any pedestrians they would have been scurrying to get across. But there weren't, so they didn't (does a falling tree on a deserted island make a noise?). Still a quarter-block away, and the amber posted itself proudly. Dick smiled—smiles of impending victory are always so much haughtier than smiles of actual victory. *Click*, red. The Chevy came to a clunking halt. Nonchalantly the driver looked both ways into the miles of barren street and then proceeded through the intersection. I declared by fiat that the bet was a tie since the driver *did* in a sense make it, and we strolled back into the air-conditioned hotel. Enough mardi gras for one night.

It had been only an hour since our plane had arrived from Dulles Airport with an intermediary stop in—God save the children—Dallas, the city where the Youth for Yarborough were considered the "underground." I was still wearing my dark-green sport coat, yellowish-brown striped tie, and parachute dress-pants. When I had walked into the office that morning I had received hoots from Sam and whistles from Marge. It was the first time they had seen me out of my sockless-moccasin ensemble.

Dick and I decided to go up to our room to change to jeans and sport shirts, but before doing so we became engaged in a conversation with the hotel clerk.

"I don't understand," I said. "El Paso has several hundred thousand people. There must be *some* things to do on a week-end night." The clerk, a Chicano, was surprised by my ignorance and a bit offended by assumptions.

"I tale you, meester. There'd be sometheen to do eef dee people had mawny to do it weeth." Instant flush, regretting as usual my initial cynicism. "Everone jus too poor." The '57

Chevy was a luxury. "But eef you wanna good time, go 'cross dee border to Juarez—only a couple block."

On the elevator up to our room Dylan's "Tom Thumb Blues" retraced its plaintive rhythm through my mind. "When you're lost in the rain in Juarez, and it's Easter time too/And your gravity fails and negativity don't pull you through. . . ." I decided to make my change of clothes to pajamas. My border crossing would wait for another night.

The next morning came the hordes, the youth peril, if you will. They came from all over the country and in all types of decanters. From the large, cosmopolitan universities came the progressives, the left-liberals, the radicals, the Beautiful People. They came with beads, beards, braids, peasant shirts, bell-bottoms, hopes, hang-ups, sandals, Marlboros, vibrance, mod watch bands, and contraceptives. They would have been a reasonably good imitation of the Atlantic City crowd, but their irrepressible senses of activism and organizing gave away the disguise. They were a genuinely good group, easy lifestyles, easy friendships. And then there was the outflanked minority, the "Bad Hundred," as I liked to call them in my moods of shallow tolerance. Some were from midwestern junior colleges, some from all-girls' or all-boys' schools in yet-to-be-discovered states. The girls came with white ruffled dresses, pageboys, and high heels, walking as though even their legs had been starched and ironed; the guys in crew cuts and fraternity shirts—all had Pepsi on their breaths. These were the Nixon Jugend. Many of them, however, didn't stay long. After a few days they left, repulsed and soured, for their campuses back home. Sometimes I fantasied that they had all been vaporized in the El Paso sun.

On this first day the representatives mingled in the hotel lobby as they registered for the congress and picked up literature from the special-interest groups, all done to the peppery beat and brass horns of the Mexican troubadours who were paid by

NSA to stand just inside the front door and play their music, and every now and then throw in an "Olé" just so we children of the elite wouldn't take them for Italians.

While the masses were forming lines to register by regions, I presented myself at the desk that gave credentials to "official observers," that is, nonvoting lobbyists. For the next two weeks this was to be Dick's and my disenfranchised status. Hawk, on the other hand, still maintained his mantle of national NSA executive. For most of the time down there he was busy leading a workshop entitled "War as a Way of Life." Among other activities, he had Seymour Hersh come down to talk about chemical and biological warfare. That day produced many reconsidering pacifists as Hersh told in detail of the army's penchant for using American C.O.'s as medical guinea pigs.

While waiting for the clerk to find my pre-registration card and name-tag (à la parents' day in grammar school), I was approached—yea, verily accosted—by a rather short, middle-aged-looking twenty-four-year-old. He not only extended his hand but, like a honing device, flawlessly found my own lathargic fingers at my side and brought them up for me to a hand-shaking position. He smiled as he gave me his name; I smiled as I gave him mine and immediately forgot his. The brownish hair atop his head looked as if it had been combed by a computer. He took the lead in the conversation but spoke in such oblique generalities that it didn't seem to be leading anywhere. First he talked about how he was excited by the "student movement"—he didn't care to specify whether that was the Young Republicans or the Weathermen. Under each category he expected me to provide my personal tastes and directions so he could continue on safe ground, but I wasn't in an obliging mood. And so he continued to speak in Roman numerals and I continued to decline to fill in the outline. It was a tête-à-tête with one of the têtes missing. After several minutes of listing topics of conversation, he finally got around to mentioning that

he was running for NSA president, and even admitted with
some prodding that it was his fourth attempt at the office.

"Good for you," I said with reception-line sincerity. At the
same time I began fastening on my name-tag—"Vietnam
Moratorium Committee, *Observer*." His words lost their previous ardor. "Just here as an observer, huh?" he asked with all
the enthusiasm of a senator who had just wasted precious minutes on a mature-looking seventeen-year-old. I apologized for not
having a vote but assured him that if I had, he wouldn't get it.
He took it with all the good humor in which it wasn't intended,
and we both had a good laugh, mine a bit heartier than his. As
the laughter dribbled into silence and coughs he excused himself and disappeared into the crowd. A real *schmuck*, that one.

The lines at registration were lengthening, and I felt like
taking a walk.

Once out on the sun-dazzled sidewalks where even the
most robust eye was whittled to a squint, I began to sense the
distrust of this foreign land. El Paso is a sultry border town,
and reluctant home of the University of Texas, El Paso Extension (a recently accepted name-change for Texas Western).
The reluctance and fear was worn by every sun-beaten, system-
beaten face in town—as they walked from store to store, but
buying little; as they crowded at the beginning and end of each
day into rickety buses that would have been auctioned or
scrapped twenty years ago in any of the cities I had known. And
the lines on the spent, enervated faces burrowed even deeper
when I or a group of us students would pass. We were a dangling reminder to these poor (mostly Chicano) of the "affluent
society." Our white skin was a reminder that some don't work
in the sun, but only rest or maybe tan in it, and our long hair
told of the leisure time we had to grow it.

But El Paso has more than just a campus. It's also the
proud father of a bastard army base—Fort Bliss, it was bap-
tized. Flourishing army bases have always seemed to be one of

the South's by-products (slag, to be sure), but at Fort Bliss, as
at other major soldier factories, a touch of Movement seems
to be in the breeze. In decades past "yes, sir" and "no, sir" were
the only utterances to be heard around the bases, but now one
listens to more and more of "gotta organize" and "see you at the
meeting." It's no longer whispered, either. Over the two weeks
I met dozens of G.I.'s who were actively organizing the antiwar,
antimilitary sentiment that was emerging from within the
barracks. They were what *Newsweek* was later to call "the new
G.I., for pot and peace." (Bob Hope, your encores are num-
bered.) One of the more active from this cadre whom I got to
know was a thirty-year-old fellow who had recently resigned
his commission as a protest against the war. He wore a neatly
trimmed, almost professorial beard and was built like a tank.

"You see, the only genuine problem," he said, looking and
even sounding a bit like Orson Welles, "is that many of the
peacenik G.I.'s think they're alone. They're afraid to say anything even to their friends." He bellowed at me from atop his
mountain chest, "So many fuckin' M.I.'s (military intelligence).
Makes the army good at psychological isolation. But that's all
ending, you see. Now we're getting wise." He stroked his beard
lovingly, his military career behind him. "You want to know
what the generals are afraid of? I was an officer and I know.
Want to know?" He glanced about with dramatic urgency and
the strong baritone timbre lowered to an emotional whisper.
"They're afraid . . . I mean, they're *really* afraid that one of
these bright, clear mornings they're going to blow that bugle
and no one, but *no* one, is going to come out and line up." The
resonance coming back to his voice now, "Don't you see? It's all
psychological. You'll fight because every one else is going to
fight, but as soon as the scales tip just so far and enough people
say 'Hell no!' then they tip all the way and the whole psychology
explodes." Hear, hear. Up the military's turkey-hole! "That's
right," he said. "It's no longer a question of 'should we?' It's a

matter of *how*; how do we most effectively fuck up the army?"
That at first seemed a big "how" to me, but not so great after
he described in some detail ways to sabotage the system. Loop-
holes in military law, ways to prevent orders from ever getting
through, ways to outsmart everything. Clever beyond belief.
It's little wonder the top bosses now want an all-volunteer army.
Taking orders just isn't as in as it used to be.

But this officer-turned-organizer wasn't my first contact
with the Texas anti-military military. No, the first was on a
street corner on this initial day of inspecting El Paso. He was a
stick of a fellow, about my age with army-short blond hair.
There he was at a main downtown intersection, both hands
wrapped in cotton and gauze, handing out as best he could
flyers that publicized a G.I. antiwar rally that was to take place
the next day in a nearby canyon. He offered me his bandaged
cotton-fluff hand, which I shook gently as I would shake a giant
Q-tip.

"Hurt your hands, huh?" I asked. My two surgery department summers trained me for such incisive observation.

"Yeah, he laughed, "ditch-diggin' will do that to 'em."

"Must have been a hell of a ditch."

He chuckled—amazingly good-spirited for a man who had
to eat with cotton clubs. "Yeah, a twenty-four-hour ditch. Bastard officer didn't take to the antiwar raps I was givin' people,
so he *suggested* I dig a little while I rap about the war. Twenty-
four straight hours, no food, no rest." He smiled as he offered
his mimeographed leaflets to the middle-aged passersby, but
they only averted their eyes or nervously turned to say something to the person with them—anything to avoid an eye-to-eye
"no, thank you." They didn't trust printed material that wasn't
in a tabloid. "That's right," he continued. "And then when they
saw my hands were all puffed and bleedin' they told me I could
spend a day in the hospital." He rotated like a top while he
spoke, trying not to miss anyone. "But you see there was this

nice little nurse who would do anything to help unstick my window, and so while she was strugglin' with it I grabbed my clothes and here I am, askin' to catch hell again." There are very few prices to be paid for being a student antiwar activist. Not everyone has that immunity.

Needless to say, I was duly impressed by his personal and defiant assault on the war and the complimentary "screw you" attitude he held for his superiors. I wouldn't have missed the rally for all the pledges in Hadassah.

The next afternoon I and a hundred other students took a bus to that rally. It was held in a canyon about ten miles outside of El Paso—a real-live Randolph Scott–Sonny Tufts canyon. We sat (several hundred of us in all) on the toasting slabs of rock, listening to speeches and songs. Most of the speeches were given by men stationed at Fort Bliss; the songs were sung by a red-headed Pfc by the name of Eddie Hodges. The same one? Indeed, the same one I had watched from a velvety Broadway seat ten years earlier in *Music Man*. But this time around he wasn't singing "Gary, Indiana," but "Lyndon Johnson Told the Nation" and "Fixin' to Die Rag." Adorable little Eddie, his voice deepened a couple of octaves, had grown a good deal larger and just a wee bit angrier over the last ten years.

And the anger wasn't singular. It churned and welled up inside of every G.I. there. It was in the rasp and resentment of every voice to come over the microphone and ricochet off the canyon rocks; it was in the tensed muscles of every shirtless soldier that sat listening. Anger. Anger over the war, what the war had already done to their personal lives and the ultimate future with which it taunted them. Anger over the manless manhood the army was trying to foist upon its captives. That's how most of the speakers viewed themselves—captives. They were American citizens but were living like rightless, medieval peasants in a small army village that was ensconced somewhere in America's blind spot. Captives without rights. Except for these collector-rare, off-base rallies, the rights of dissent are army mythology. Even as the bitter words trailed off into the canyon gorges two men with a telescope and pencil stood atop a cliff that overlooked the rally site. Perhaps a corny imitation of 1984, but the military intelligence has never worried itself over its reviews. They were taking names, and they wanted everyone to know they were taking names. Another reminder that my memory will always be preserved (and immortality assured) in police microfilm—my genes may now do as they please.

After the rally one of the dissident leaders pointed to the afternoon as evidence of growing antiwar feelings among G.I.'s and chided me for the lack of interest in G.I. organizing shown by groups like the Moratorium Committee. My civilian buttocks rightfully spanked, we agreed to set up a meeting within the next couple of days to get Moratorium plans going at Fort Bliss. At that meeting Dave, Dick, and I outlined the various activities being planned for October 15 on the campuses and made some suggestions for actions to be taken on the army base. Most of the men there were college graduates and bitterly anti-army. Their impromptu leader, a Vietnam veteran, was the most willing to chance punishment. The several times after the meeting that he apologized for the less bold I squirmed with discomfort (easy-street student guilt?). Of course G.I.'s aren't free like students to take any given day off for rallies and community canvassing, but even the more reluctant ones promised that if nothing else, come mid-October, sick bay would be an incredibly popular hang-out at Fort Bliss.

The schedules at NSA congresses run something like Las Vegas time, beginning at noon and ending at three or four in the morning. Each afternoon there would be workshops ad infinitum that one could attend if he so desired. The subjects of the workshops varied all the way from Hawk's "War as a

Way of Life" to "Educational Reform" to Bill Baird's workshop on birth control. Baird was the object of a famous Supreme Court test case on the matter after he had publicly (in Boston no less) given birth control information and devices to unmarrieds. Because his information table at the congress had been set up next to ours, I heard hour upon hour and afternoon upon afternoon his talks about birth control. Condoms, coils, diaphragms, foams, jellies, pills—he had it all down pat. He talked about everything to do with sex except sex. I was bored to tears.

There was one afternoon, however, when Hawk, Dick, and I were able to break away from the workshop-organize script and spend a few hours at the University of Texas pool, a time of relaxation I mercilessly exaggerated over the phone to Sam and Marge, who were back in Swelter City.

"How are things going down there?" Sam would ask in a more-than-usual business manner.

"Just as smoothly as could be," I answered, "although the water *is* a bit tepid in the afternoon."

At night most of the time was taken up with the NSA plenaries, the mass meetings in the university gymnasium to decide the future NSA policies and elect the coming year's officers. Great pains were taken to simulate the national party fiascoes that occur every four years. The schools were assigned space on the "convention floor" according to state, each table with a standard bearing the name of that state. Throughout the speeches, points of order, objections, clarifications, amendments, et cetera, et cetera, it was my job to roam the aisles (à la Lyndon Johnson, the Senate Majority Leader) to talk about the war, the possibility of a mass NSA action such as the "Dump Johnson" movement of 1967, to get names, connections, commitments to begin organizing on home campuses—in general to whisper in ears about the thing that we all eventually scream at each other through microphones. My buttonholing style, however, was as yet unpolished. Names were never my forte—I've been known to forget my brother's—this always tends to deflate an otherwise buoyant handshake and smile. Nor was my "let's talk it over" pose perfected. From what I see and read the idea is to casually bend down over the delegate like a father helping with his son's homework, impale the listener with a strong, piercing first line, pause tantalizingly to listen to what the speaker at the podium is saying, and then assume the classic squat next to the conventioneer's chair to dig in the final barbs of verbal intercourse. At that point, on my haunches, I would often as not lose my balance and fall over, detracting considerably from the gravity of my dialogue. But despite these occasional faux pas, it all seemed to be turning out as planned. In one way or another, interest in a national Vietnam protest was being generated. One could just feel that the time was right for the campuses to move again. Whatever else happened, the colleges would be striking on October 15.

One of the attractive and reaffirmative dimensions of speaking to these new people—people who were beyond the orb of the Moratorium office—was that the conversation constantly pivoted about the core and fountainhead of all the anger, the frustration, the reason for taking action—namely, the war in Vietnam. Though it may sound ludicrous, this simply wasn't the case inside the walls of the protest office itself. Only on rare occasions in the office did that subject, that war come to the surface. Usually it was shuttled and sifted and ultimately buried beneath the tumultuous machinery of day-to-day organizing. It was easy alchemy to turn the traces of ideologue in each of us to unadulterated pragmatist. In the office the time was necessarily taken up with trying to persuade so-and-so to give a speech or endorsement, or the logistics of setting up a rally, or seeing that the next mailing got out. It wasn't by design but by necessity. One of the last times I had actually discussed the war with a fellow organizer was during my visit with Sam months earlier at the Kennedy Institute. But that had been my last glimpse at the forest—the guiding trees since then were the mimeograph machine, the letters, the phone messages, the money solicitations, the contact sheets. The cumbersome bureaucracy is of course necessary if anything is to be accomplished, but at the same time it is a dangerous course the individual takes when he is willing to accept more and more as *a priori* that needn't be discussed anymore. It stultifies and it can eventually distort. In time you're merely organizing, not consciously for or against *anything*. History may show that it's against the war and you may sense that it's against the war, but at times your mind wonders and is boggled by it all.

Our conventioning Moratorium rap wasn't without complications. As has already been mentioned, the Moratorium Committee was engaged in a tightrope walk between the liberal and radical factions of the antiwar movement, hoping it could stick to a narrow enough platform to avoid alienating either side. And as has also been mentioned, one of the most outspoken antiwar congressmen, Allard Lowenstein from New York, was declining to support the Moratorium because of its refusal to condemn campus radicals, and was in fact attempting to build out of his own Congressional office a liberal campus movement that would overtake campus radicalism. "As unfortunate as it might be," Lowenstein used to say, "we must accept even a Ronald Reagan before we can accept SDS." Given this snatch of history, the dilemma for us stemmed from the fact that the most popular candidate for NSA president at this convention was a twenty-five-year-old black by the name of Clinton Deveaux, once referred to in the *New York Times* as "Allard Lowenstein's protegé." Deveaux, a slim, soft-spoken fellow who was progressive enough to not be taken as anyone's Uncle Tom but totally committed to nonviolence (had received a C.O. from the military), was at the time working as a staffer in

Lowenstein's Washington office. Many of those who know him claim he will be the first black U.S. president if Julian Bond doesn't beat him to it. Had he merely been a Lowenstein (and thus an anti-Moratorium Committee) force, matters might have been simple enough. But as antiwar politics would have it, Deveaux was also a personal friend of Sam, Marge, and David (Mixner).

It was indeed a well-knit rub. The last thing the Moratorium needed, if it were going to succeed on the campuses, was an NSA president who couldn't support the protest. But then again, who was going to politic against a personal friend of half the Moratorium staff? Certainly not this friction-avoider. The only solution for us three lobbyists was to dodge as well as possible any role in the fight for NSA president, but instead to just hope for some type of upset. There was in fact this possibility with the entrance into the race of Charlie Palmer, former student-body president at Berkeley and scenario writer of the People's Park drama. Quiet hoorays from us for the new candidate.

But our cheers weren't needed. Deveaux was virtually eliminated as a presidential contender during one of the last plenaries of the convention. It started as the night to begin consideration of the following year's officers, but ended as a bizarre evening that touched on far more important matters than the NSA presidency.

That whole week tension had been building between the majority white membership and the "Third World Caucus," a coalition of black and Chicano delegates. The Caucus had been holding separate meetings in lieu of the scheduled NSA activities. Several days earlier I had accidentally stumbled upon one such meeting that had been hastily assembled on the eighth floor of the Cortez Hotel. I was on my way to visit a delegate-friend from Radcliffe whom I had just met (a short and awkward affair that only an El Paso hotel two thousand miles from

home could harbor). Stepping out of the elevator, I was caught
on the chin by sixty pair of unwelcoming eyes. Sinking, oh that
Palisades Park sinking sensation! My solar plexus churned, "Not
for you, white boy." My brain whispered in reply, "I know.
Jesus Christ, I know." No one spoke—the meeting couldn't
continue. With a precision pivot that one rarely sees even at the
changing of the guard, I turned every huddled white cell of my
body around and stepped back into the elevator. I'd pay a visit
another time.

Two days later came a verbal clash between some of the
Chicano and white students in the hotel lobby. All during the
congress attention had been drawn to constructing some type
of action against the local one-percent sales tax that was being
used to build a new civic center rather than to help the more
than twenty-five thousand Chicano who lived in the pre-
Dickensian squalor on the south end of the city. This particular
afternoon several white NSA'ers had been arrested for staging a
sit-in in one of the El Paso restaurants and refusing to pay the
sales tax. One of the Chicano cops who had to clear everyone
out told me before going into the restaurant, "Don't whorry,
no whunz going to be hurt. Zaven years I've had thees club,
whun scratch." He pointed to a lonely indentation half-way
down his billy club. "An' that whuz from tryheen to zeparate
two cars."

But the younger Chicano at the convention had no such
lack of hostility for the whites who had staged the sit-in. They
charged that the whites had gone ahead as usual with an action
without consulting the people it was intended to help. "We're
the leaders of the Chicano movement, not you," one of them
barked from atop a chair in the hotel lobby. Then one of the
female black leaders climbed the impromtu podium (with her
leg in a cast it took some assistance). "White people like to
co-opt poor people's problems," she said, "and then become
martyrs." Few of the whites there defended the sit-in. Most just

stared at the ground and made patterns in the lobby carpet with
their feet, perhaps looking for Texas herbs to salve their chafed
liberalism. When the meekly accepted chastisement was over,
the wounded white activists shuffled back up to their rooms.
Had I been black I think I would have been offended by it all
as being one of the worst imitations of Stepin Fetchit ever
attempted. As it was, I was only white, therefore irrelevant and
offended.

No, things hadn't been going swimmingly between the
races, and this night's plenary didn't bode better times. The
evening, like the evenings before and after it, was hot and
desert dry. Almost all the delegates were on hand. As was the
custom of these sessions the business at hand was preceded by
an address from an invited speaker. Tonight the speaker was
Muhammed Kenyatta, a barrel-chested, dashikied black man
who had been working with James Forman in seeking $500
million in "reparations" from American churches. Churches,
however, weren't Kenyatta's only target, at least not this night.
He wanted NSA to, first, pass a resolution condemning itself
as a racist organization (a rather fastidious way to beat one's
breast, don't you think?) and secondly, give half the money it
had ever spent on civil rights projects from 1960 on (and half
of its coming budget) to black students to be used in all further
anti-racist programs. The majority, however, weren't about to
approve those two demands, but Kenyatta was in no particular
hurry—he was prepared to remain on the speaker's platform
until the resolution *was* passed.

At this point, Robert Powell, the present NSA president,
who was presiding over the plenaries with all the energy and
enthusiasm required of the job, stepped back up to the microphone to explain that no resolutions could be considered until
the officers for next year were elected but that it could be
brought up at the following night's meeting. Kenyatta, visibly

angered, left the stage and walked out of the gymnasium, followed by about sixty black students.

Powell, now siphoned of some of his enthusiasm, contined with the meeting. The hyperbole and platitudes of the nomination speeches were yet to be made. Now was the time. Friends and sycophants streamed past the microphone to test their oratory. I hadn't viewed such an unmoved audience since the speech at the 1968 Republican Convention to nominate Harold Stassen. Meanwhile, in the halls outside, the Third World Caucus held its own meeting.

Asking for a point of order, one of the delegates from Syracuse University rose and, before Powell could react, launched into one of the finest imitations of Richard Nixon since David Fry. "I just want to make one thing crystal clear," he snorted from somewhere deep in his esophagus, "this whole proceeding is totally irrelevant." Hoots and cheers. "Now I understand you young people and I'm sure you'll agree with me that these nomination speeches are irrelevant as well." He rubbed his carefully grown stubble. "And I'm going to be quite candid with you now." His suspiciously darting eyes brought more whistles of approval. "I'm the most irrelevant of all." Thunderous applause. He took his seat, then rose again to the ovation, and finally mounted the New York table and with both hands raised in "V" acknowledged the squealing masses. When black delegates and white interest leave a meeting, absurdity is a sure filler.

The gavel rapped. Powell, smothering his own laughter, brought the meeting back to religious order. The speeches would continue. I sat in the bleachers along with the reporters and the other "official observers" with my elbows on my knees and my chin in my hands. Just before I was asphyxiated by the verbiage, the black contingent re-entered the gymnasium. Determination entered with them. Upon the conclusion of the speech, one of the black students toward the front rose to one of the floor mikes, asking for a point of order.

"It seems clear to us," he began, "that this racist convention just doesn't want to face up to its own responsibilities." Powell rapped his gavel and told the speaker that he was out of order. Resolutions would be considered the next night. "Now you listen to me, man," the objector continued, "don't give me any of your parliamentary bullshit. Black people are suffering all over this country, so let's you and me get down to some *real* business." Troubled eyebrows spread across the faces in the hall. The great white guilt, a mammoth glacier, had budged its annual quarter inch.

Powell paused and leaned on the lectern in the middle of the stage, searching for the diplomatic path. "The chair must rule you out of order"—the words creaked with the inanimateness of an actual chair—"but I can put it to a vote to see if the meeting wishes to overrule the chair." There was a general snicker from the blacks—parliamentary bullshit, excreted from the bowels of Western Europe. "All those in favor of hearing the speaker from the floor?" A couple of hundred *ayes*. "Opposed?" Twice as many *nays*. The glacier had crept back unseen. The black student stood with hands on hips, nudging the sides of his sportcoat to the rear. "Bullshit!" was the last thought he cared to make public through the microphone. He turned and walked away, but not before shoving the standing floor-mike so it rocked on its base like a plastic clown with a lead-filled bottom. A viscous silence glutted the convention hall.

Another hand from the floor. A genuine point of order? No, just our friend from Syracuse with another round of Nixon. Nothing like humor to ease tensions *and* avoid the problem. "You're out of order," Powell said unhesitatingly. That was followed by boos and a refrain of "let him speak." "All right," said Powell, "we'll put it to a vote again." *This* time the chair was overruled—Nixon could speak. Well, that just about did it.

In the middle of the comic's routine the same fellow who had so recently left the mike dizzy with reeling returned to the scene of the crime. "Man, this says it all," he screamed. Our comic stopped short. "We got something serious to talk about, but that's out of order. But the fuckin' funny man you whites'll listen to all day!" Powell was trapped. He had played it by the book and now he was trapped. "You're out of order," he said, trying to muster all the calmness his voice still owned. Good Lord, couldn't he have at least used some other phrase?!

"I'll show you who's out of order!" the black student spit back. With that he picked up the closest table marker (it happened to be the standard bearing "Wyoming") and smashed it on the edge of the stage. Wooden splinters flew everywhere. No more Roberts' Rules for tonight. Some of the white students at the Wyoming table eased themselves out of their chairs and began back-peddling away from the scene but always keeping an eye on the wooden stump that was now being waved in the air. The seething brandisher returned to the microphone, his voice now trembling with emotion. "Don't you motherfuckers go telling me what's a point of——" The sentence was never finished. The mike had been turned off from the control booth that hung above the gymnasium floor. At that the fellow dropped his wooden sword and with both hands wrenched the mike from its floor moorings. Its long cord whipped with the yank and snared in the legs of nearby chairs. That was only a sample. It was followed by half a dozen blacks stalking the aisles and hurling the remaining floor mikes to the ground, ripping metal from cord. The wail of jostled electricity screeched and crackled through the speakers, and finally went silent. There would be no more points of order tonight. Now only the stage mike worked.

A couple of dozen whites headed for the doors but found they had been locked from the outside—seven or eight blacks stood on the other side to make sure they remained locked.

Within seconds the message of "we're locked in" spread from one end of the gym to the other. That, I thought, would be the final catalyst, the spark in a fume-filled room. But no, the whites were not about to challenge the guards at the doors, at least not for the moment.

High in the rafters in the meantime the fellow in the control booth was signaling to compatriots on the floor—together they would try to restore the damaged parts of the sound system. But he didn't have long to do it. Two black students running along the catwalks were closing in on the booth from opposite directions. We watched with labored breath from below. Visions of someone falling seventy feet to the hardwood floor below pillaged my mind. The mike operator, now seeing for the first time his approaching guests, stepped back from the buttons and switches—he had no appetite for a cliff scene. What transpired in that brief aerial conference I don't know, but when it was over the white student left and the black students stayed in the booth.

Meanwhile on stage there was more juggling of tempers. Only one mike, but two claimants. One was the president, Powell, a jumbo but decidedly noncombative fellow, who stood with one hand in his pocket, the other hand scratching the back of his neck. The other was an equally stocky black student. His voice couldn't be heard by most in the hall, but his gestures were making it clear he was incensed. Then with one hand and little effort he hurled the lectern off the stage. The wooden lectern met the floor with an earsplitting crash. One girl who didn't see it fall thought it was gunfire and screamed. The dislodging of the lectern snagged the criss-cross of wires and now had the microphone dangling eight feet off the ground. The candidate, Charlie Palmer, standing on a chair, began speaking through it, trying to talk some sense into everyone before it was too late. "All right, now the first thing I think we all have to do is just keep our . . ." The voice trailed off, and one of the new occupiers of the control booth smiled—his fingers had found new and exciting power. Palmer stepped down from the deadened microphone. He was the only candidate who even attempted to put his election on the line this night. Deveaux, the "black moderate" had quietly left the gym just before the doors were locked. The next day he charged he had been threatened by some of the blacks who had taken over the meeting. No matter—his chances for the presidency had exited with him that night.

So there we all were—locked in, lectern and chairs strewn along the floor, fists still clenched, the one operable mike silenced by its protectors, emotions tense and ominous. No one knew what the next move might be. People only sat at their tables, fingers drumming, or wandered nervously about the gym. No one knew if it was the aftermath or only the beginning. We were stalled, like a ball precariously perched on the fulcrum of a see-saw. Odds were the only rational basis for speculation. Eventually the ball would begin rolling again, and with the tipping of the board in one direction it would gain more and more momentum until the see-saw would finally touch ground at one end or the other. Exponential destiny. But still no one knew which end it would be, the restoration of calm or total explosion. People breathed with economy.

Several minutes passed. The only sound was the murmurings of scattered private conversations. Another minute passed, then another. And with each minute one could hear a more distinct creaking of the see-saw. The ball had begun its roll toward calm—enough time had passed for the people to again slide out in front of events. Now several of the whites who had been conducting the meeting were talking quietly with Kenyatta. The microphone on the stage was being rehabilitated so Kenyatta might give a short speech to bring the meeting full swing back to systematized politics—it would come to a vote, not a brawl. His speech was short and to the point. He reiterated his belief that NSA, like most institutions in this country, had a debt to pay black people. The whites were either with the blacks or they were against them—a vote would decide. I was thankful I didn't have a vote to cast—I don't know which way it would have gone. My general sympathies were with the black demands, but I resented the Cleaveresque logic of there being only two sides to the world, the problem and the solution, each person being one or the other. I resented someone's trying to make my world that simplistic. It placed me in the position of either acceding to every demand ever issued by a black group or being "racist." The conclusion of Kenyatta's demand may have been sound, but the reasoning grated. I was glad to be an observer.

My vote, however, wouldn't have really mattered. It was a considerable majority (two-thirds, probably) that voted against Kenyatta's demand. The only thing left for the black students was to announce that they were breaking away from NSA and forming a National Association of Black Students, more evidence that we weren't living in a polarized society but indeed in two separate societies (somehow we never realize it until visibly separate institutions punctuate the fact). The blacks left the gymnasium, this time calmly and with deliberation, this time at least with an answer, perhaps even a satisfaction of a type.

The next night Charlie Palmer was elected president, Clint Deveaux vice president. Few blacks were on hand. The subject of race at this convention had passed its moment. It had been supplanted by the question of the war, which for these delegates was more of a rhetorical question than anything else. The Moratorium was supported unanimously at this last plenary—approved by acclamation. The stragglers of the "Bad Hundred" must have abstained (a very silent minority!). The difference in reactions to the war and racism came as no surprise to me (probably because my own reactions came as no surprise). The white students couldn't always feel the oppression in this country, but they *could* feel the war.

On the plane back to Washington the next morning I began reading a book by Lawrence Wittner entitled *Rebels Against War*. I would use it for my senior thesis on the Moratorium in the fall. Like most other books about the antiwar movement in this country's history, it drew attention to the fact that although there has always been a good deal of antiwar sentiment among blacks, that sentiment has seldom been converted into genuine antiwar activism. The wars have always been white upper-middle-class issues. Upper-middle-class whites were the ones who ran them, and they were the ones who actively opposed them. From this convention I was beginning to understand the blacks' thinking on the matter. The wealthy white kids would always be there to protest a war. The wars touched, if not their own interests (which they usually *did*), then certainly their awareness. I, like them, could clearly tell someone more of the horrors of Vietnam than of Harlem. But the blacks know both wars, and if they were to spend time organizing against the wars abroad, who would be there to wage *their* battle at home? I felt as though I were helplessly becoming part of another as yet unwritten chapter to Wittner's book. The Moratorium, it seemed, would be like the antiwar movements before it, essentially white, quintessentially wealthy.

CHAPTER FOUR

"I'd rather be a Duchess than a Dutch,
But not much."
—BLUECOLLAR FEMINISTS' MANIFESTO

I sat on the pier in the slowly cooling September sun, my feet playfully poking at the rippled water. The waves poked right back and gently chided me for not being around during the warmer, more summery days that were now gone for another year. A small cloud, one of those little foreign jobs, passed quickly overhead, and for a shadow's moment I could feel the chill of an approaching autumn. It had been only three days since I left El Paso, only one day since I returned to Washington, cleaned up the residue of paperwork, and taken off for a week's stay at my parents' summer cottage in Wisconsin. It was September 4—soon it would be too cold to swim.

Marcie was back from Europe, and we had spoken several times over the phone. I hadn't been erased in Europe after all, just temporarily suspended. That's what she said, and that's what I hoped was true. It seemed that *maybe* we could begin things where we had left them. In another couple of weeks we could see and hold each other again, and maybe then we would know.

Cedar Lake seemed for many reasons to be the logical place to spend these few private days. In just a short time I would be returning to Cambridge to finish my last year of college, but, more important, to begin organizing the campuses in New England for the Moratorium. October 15 was the first target date, but if everything went well that would be just the start. Each month the Moratorium would expand one day—hopefully it would grow into a full national strike. For me that meant months of being with people and more people—convincing, cajoling, arguing, organizing, stopping for lunch, and more organizing. There would be little time in the near future to just sit and think and be human.

And so we lingered, Cedar Lake and I, over each moment we could still spend together. I leaned back and looked toward the other end of the pier that was firmly anchored in the sand and rock. The oak trees in front of our cottage breathed a hint of red and orange, and even the mint leaves along the shore showed a bit of arthritic pain from the recent industrious night air. The lake and I had each passed some ineffable, intuitively significant marker in our respective lives. The long, hard push lay ahead for us both.

"Ken," I heard someone shout from several hundred feet away. "There's a call for you." It was my father standing at the top of the stone stairs that lead from the shore to our cottage. Ah yes, the phone, the nagging bitch of my life. I conquered the incline three steps at a time and picked up the receiver in the front porch.

"Mr. Ken Hurwitz, please?" A pleasantly un-nasal operator.

"Yeah, right."

"Go ahead, Washington."

"Ken this is Hawk." Self-reference by surname had always been a curiosity to me. An eye on history? A way of objectifying one's life? A lack of self-intimacy, perhaps? "How's your vacation goin'?" he asked with not too much interest.

"Just fine, Dave, what's up?" The phone call had me a bit bewildered. My work in the Washington office had been wrapped up on that last day between El Paso and Wisconsin. Sam and Dave and I had agreed then that I would be the New England campus coordinator and work out of Cambridge. Dick would be concentrating on the Middle Atlantic states, and new staffers were being brought in to divide up the rest of our old territories. I wasn't enthusiastic about shifting from western campuses to the ones in New England—it meant a whole new set of names and places with which to familiarize myself—nor was I particularly happy about leaving the Washington office to return to school, but I had little choice in the matter. My local draft board has yet to give a deferment for antiwar organizing.

"Well, how would you like to do a little Midwest gig for the Moratorium?" Hawk asked. On-the-road organizing. How those last moments of summer can vanish!

"Sure thing, what's the deal?" Hawk then proceeded to outline exactly what had to be done. I was to board a plane in Milwaukee early the next week and in a two-day span visit three midwestern cities—Indianapolis, St. Louis, and Kansas City. I would travel with Stuart Meacham, head of the American Friends' Service Committee (AFSC) and one of the cochairmen along with David Dellinger and several others of the New Mobilization Committee, the group that was planning a march on Washington for November 15. Together Meacham and I were to outline to local antiwar leaders the so-called Fall Offensive. That was the term used to incorporate the Moratorium's October 15 and Mobilization's November 15 dates. During those same few days other representatives from the Moratorium Committee and the New Mobe would be going to other major cities all around the country for the same purpose. It would be the largest, most extravagant organizing effort the two antiwar groups would pursue conjunctively. Hawk called it "the flying circus."

"Now listen," Hawk said. "Meacham knows the ropes, so let him take the lead. OK?"

"Uh, huh, sure."

"And of course don't discourage anyone from going to Washington in November." I didn't say anything. Hawk knew I didn't particularly care for the potentially violent weekend the Mobilization was planning, but being on the Mobe's steering committee, he wanted to make sure I wasn't about to create additional friction between the two groups. "Just tell the local organizers that whoever can get to Washington in November should go, and whoever can't can continue locally with Moratorium activities." There was an edge of impatience in his voice.

"Yeah . . . well, OK, I guess." I figured I could talk to the people about October and not say anything either way about November. "Everything else is all set, the plane tickets will be waiting for you at the Milwaukee airport, and the meetings in all the cities have been arranged. From Kansas City you'll come back to Washington—it'll give us a chance to talk over final plans for a day before you go back to school. OK?"

"Yeah, OK, Dave, see you in a week." *Click.* Somehow I just couldn't see myself flying from city to city for prearranged meetings. That was something for company execs and big time pols, not for me. Someday, I suppose, I'll stop differentiating between me and "grownups," but until then the best I can do in these situations is make believe.

And so within a week I was on my way for a two-and-a-half-day stint of local organizing. All around the country other Mobe and Moratorium leaders were doing the same. This was the beginning of a sometimes rankling, sometimes congenial, but *always* confusing relationship between the two protest groups.

The Mobilization's march in Washington was set for November 15; the two days of local Moratorium activities for that month were scheduled for November 14 and 15. Most of the public never really did differentiate between the two organizations. All through Washington on the November 15 weekend I saw police traffic signs that read, "Moratorium buses, use right lane," and I still hear friends mention the "November Moratorium in Washington." Not so, I try to tell them. Different groups, different histories.

The Mobe had, like the Phoenix, been resurrected from its own smoldering ashes. It was in early July at a national antiwar conference in Cleveland that the old *National* Mobilization Committee to End the War in Vietnam was dissolved and the *New* Mobilization Committee to End the War in Vietnam was founded. A barely-changed name with barely-changed faces. The New Mobe was to be an umbrella group for all the antiwar organizations in the country and from that position to coordinate the mid-November march in Washington. Groups within that umbrella ranged all the way from the American Friends' Service Committee and our own Vietnam Moratorium Committee to the American Communist Party and the Socialist Workers' Party. In all, over eighty groups were represented.

Clearly, the New Mobe was somewhere to the left of our group. The old McCarthy and Kennedy forces, the broth of the Moratorium Committee, were a slightly less than detectable seasoning in their group. Their leaders were more oriented toward civil disobedience (many had helped engineer the 1967 March on the Pentagon) and, as became evident by November, they were far less enamored of dove politicians and labor leaders than were most Moratorium organizers. I got on the plane in Milwaukee with many doubts about the coming two days. I didn't quite know what to expect from this first contact with the New Mobe.

When I got to the motel in Indianapolis I met Stuart

Meacham, as assertively dignified, silver-haired gentleman, a father-figure from the instant we shook hands. All my worries over organizing alongside him vanished. He wrapped his large hand about my own and told me he was pleased every time he saw young people willing to work against the war nonviolently. Beneath all the calcifying years of work and frustration he still had the gentleness of youthful idealism. He was a gentle man with a gentle vision of the world to come. He wasn't working against this war because of politics or economics. He was against the war in Vietnam because he was against *all* wars.

But idealism alone isn't enough to gain one a position of leadership in the antiwar movement. It takes a good, tough ability to organize as well. Meacham has it. It seemed that every other moment, whether we were having lunch in our motel or waiting for our next plane, he was excusing himself to phone in messages to his AFSC headquarters in Philadelphia or his New Mobe headquarters in Washington. He had his fingers in nearly every antiwar project in the country, and he didn't consider himself above a little nonviolent arm twisting every now and then when things got tight. He was an idealist, not a pushover.

His decades of activism had carried him to dozens of countries. He was an internationalist, a peace broker. Over dinner with our Quaker hosts in Indianapolis he told of his time spent in Hanoi.

"I can recall getting into a jeep with one of the North Vietnamese for a trip through the countryside." His soft voice had the subtle vestiges of a one-time Alabama pastor's drawl. "As I sat in the front seat waiting to go, the man began loading an entire arsenal of rifles and hand grenades in the back. I told him that as a pacifist it was against my beliefs to arm myself." The rest of the Quakers at the table, all young, all committed pacifists, sat in uneasy attention, not at all sure they wanted to hear the fate of their religious principles in the field. "He turned to me," Meacham continued, "and said that if we were ambushed I could do whatever I pleased but that he wasn't about to get himself killed." Meacham smiled gently to himself, his fingers resting lightly on the white tablecloth. "Well, I went along in the jeep, but only God knows what I would have done if we *had* been ambushed. I can only say what I *hope* I would have done." Our hosts looked puzzled, not at all sure whether this national pacifist figure was buttressing or dismantling their religious beliefs. They wanted to hear more than just what he *hoped* he would have done. But for me, a person whose mind was still unresolved, one who was still in the process of investigating pacifism and his own soul to learn if the two might survive together, the "confession" was an instruction, not a challenge.

Meacham cupped the palms of his hands together, a fatherly as well as a clerical gesture. "And you know, when we got back safely, I asked the man if he was religious, and he answered that if wanting more than anything else in the whole world to destroy the planes and pilots that came each day to bomb his village were religion, then, yes, he was a religious man." Meacham's eyes fell vacantly on the soft, clean tablecloth and the fresh food it held, his visions ten thousand miles away in the burning flesh and foliage of Vietnam. "I didn't know what to tell him—I just didn't know what to say." His eyes glistened. "This man saw his wife and children torn apart by American bombs. Was I supposed to tell him that preventing these planes from coming again and killing his neighbors would be murder?" He looked at us, but our eyes were all on the floor. "What was I to tell that man?" Only spiritless forks on dishware broke the next hour's silence.

The morning meeting in Indianapolis was held in a second-floor seminar room of the city's new Ecumenical Center. Because Meacham had arranged the meetings, most of the orga-

nizers present were inveterate AFSC'ers, Quakers in their fifties
and sixties who had been at this antiwar thing long before I was
born. The women were in frumpish, old-fashioned dresses and
the men came in baggy work pants. Many had come in from
farms as far as seventy-five miles away, and nearly all had a hick
Hoosier accent. Corny, guileless, these were the Quakers, the
stubborn lot of America that has never had much use for what
the Eastern Establishment would call political sophistication.
Bringing food and medicine to disaster victims, resettling war
refugees, negotiating mutual releases of war prisoners, the ob-
stinate Quakers have for decades been undoing the knots the
rest of the world has tied. One old-timer, who bore some resem-
blance to the fellow on the Puffed Rice box, wrapped his
weighty arm around my shoulders to pull me into his chest, and
told me with a wink he thought my generation was doing just
fine, too.

These people had seen many antiwar projects come and go.
Many of those projects seemed thoughtful and worthwhile to
them; others were just childish or gratuitous plans for counter-
violence. They would have no part of the latter. They worked
against the war with steadiness and determination. They knew
that as soon as one problem was solved there would always be
another. All of them had been around too long to be diverted
by the manic soaring and crashing that we unseasoned activists
suffer. They never became disillusioned because they never
succumbed to illusions in the first place.

When Meacham finished explaining the planned march in
Washington, most sitting around the table reacted with reluctance. Some stared into the empty center of the table's Formica
surface, some pairs of eyes skittered sheepishly from neighbor to
silent neighbor. The basic idea was acceptable, but they just
didn't know how many could afford to charter buses and planes
to carry them that distance for a single weekend. By the time
it was my turn to explain the idea of the Moratorium, Meacham

had pushed himself back from the table, visibly disappointed at this initial reaction.

Unlike the Mobilization's plans for a centralized march, the idea of local Moratorium action met unanimous approval. They heard my description of an escalating national strike and their eyes twinkled.

"Just let us know where to start!" one sixty-five-year-old retired farmer said as he jumped up from his seat and clapped his hands.

"Well, if you had been reading their letters, you old fogey," an elderly woman who was knitting in the corner chastised, "you'd *know* where to start." Everyone laughed. "I've already contacted the mayor in my town for a parade permit, the two pastors are planning a special memorial service, and we've got ourselves a dozen high school students running off those fact sheets we got from Washington—you know, the ones with the tax dollar cut like a pie."

"But ——"

"No *buts*, old man," Grandma said. "Just do it." Then she resumed her knitting.

The farmer told me to have those organizing memos in his mailbox by the end of the week, then folded his arms and sat down.

There were other people in the room who already knew about the Moratorium, and they all competed amiably for who could boast the most work already done. One man had begun calling all the sympathetic World War II veterans he knew for a separate "veterans' vigil," and another woman was trying to organize a blood drive that would send blood to both the North and South Vietnamese. She pushed at her graying hair as though she were mad at it. "At least if it's blood you give to that Thieu and Ky," she said, "you know they can't spend it on Cadillacs." Most of the meeting I just sat and listened. They were way ahead of me.

For the first time I was out of Washington, and with grass-roots community activists on their home ground. I was out there in the proverbial heartland of America just listening, listening to their ideas and marking their reactions. It was a good feeling, a feeling that doesn't come over the phone. These midwesterners were finished hibernating; they were ready for action, and the Moratorium was just what they were looking for. These weren't "wild-eyed impatient firebrands." Nixon had told them he had a "plan for peace" but that he couldn't tell anyone what it was. Now they saw why he couldn't tell anyone, and they were ready to take action. This was only the first city I saw, but already I was sensing that perhaps something very big was burgeoning beneath our feet. I felt that maybe, just *maybe*, a genuine Movement was unfolding.

But everyone knows that movements these days don't exist without the interest of the news media. Making that political judgment was easy. Shooting my mouth off to the press every available opportunity was even easier. It was all very novel and heady. Back in Washington I had always sat comfortably off to the side while Sam volleyed questions and answers with the reporters. But now I was on my own, and I was expected for these two days to be the definitive spokesman for the Moratorium. "It's easy," I said to myself.

"It's not that easy," Meacham cautioned me as we entered our first press conference. "Just try to remember the kind of first impression you want to make on the people watching."

The room we entered was strewn with tripods and wires, and at the front was a long rectangular table with two lonely folding chairs. No pastries, no stack of press releases at the door. Very bush league compared to Brown's Hilton affairs. The TV reporter motioned us to the front of the room and told us to make ourselves "comfy." I didn't like him. He was the self-assured, navy-blue-blazer type. Slicked black hair and a little tin American flag on his lapel. Rather than ever saying "yes," he would say "righto" and point with his forefinger and thumb in the shape of a toy gun. He probably did the eleven o'clock weather report as well.

"All right, I guess we're 'bout ready to roll," he said. "Both you gentlemen ready?" We nodded. The room's walls dissolved in floodlight as the reporter turned his made-up face to the whirring movie camera. He introduced the two of us and then began by asking Meacham about the November weekend in Washington. Stuart explained with as much charm and appeal as could be the three major events for that weekend. First, the single-file march past the White House beginning Thursday night with each of over forty thousand persons carrying the name of a killed American G.I. or a decimated Vietnamese village; then, the Saturday morning march down Pennsylvania Avenue; and, third, the culminating mass rally that afternoon at the Washington Monument. All the while he outlined the Mobe's plans, the reporter was winking at the sound man. Both were profoundly unimpressed, and I was beginning to feel a good, healthy hostility for them.

Meacham finished, and the reporter shifted his eyes toward me. I could hear the camera swivel on its tripod.

"Mr. Hurwitz"—the "Mr." seemed to grate in his throat—"could you tell us a little about this Vietnam Moratorium." He pronounced the syllables precisely, as one does when he is learning a new word.

This was it, my first chance to help shape the Moratorium's public image. I brushed the longer strands of hair from my eyes, welded my feet squarely to the floor, and looked boldly into the Cyclops eye of the camera. No one in the room could have imagined how my underpants were beginning to stick.

"The reason we call this protest a moratorium and not a strike," I began, "is to make it clear that there will be no forcible actions. People will be asked to *voluntarily* cease from 'business as usual.'" This was Indiana, Nixon country, and any antiwar conversion I might make would require gently moderate baptismal water. Inflammatory rhetoric wasn't my style, anyway. I acknowledged that it is difficult to ask a worker to give up an increasing number of days' wages, but that if this strike —oops, moratorium—meant an end to the war, it would ultimately be in his interest to do so. The average-income man was paying over eight hundred dollars a year to the war, and was of course being hurt terribly by the war's resulting inflation. Clearly, the economic facts were on our side. Moreover, I emphasized, all of the protest activities would be within the law. "We don't want the issue of the war," I said, "obscured by a lesser issue such as civil disobedience."

The reporter clasped his hands behind his head and straightened his legs, tilting his chair away from the table. "Don't you think, given the public's reaction to campus violence, that the Moratorium might be counterproductive?"

I couldn't believe it. He hadn't listened to a word I had said. Why is it so ingrained in people that any campus-initiated dissent is "campus *violence*"? I knew that most people felt that way, that most people watching probably hadn't listened to a word I had said either. I was furious. If anyone were responsible for the misinterpretation of much campus dissent, it was the news media, the people who are paid to make political differentiations clear to the public. The question stripped me of any cool I might have had. My answer was defensive and argumentative. It was a disaster. My hair kept falling in my face until I couldn't even see the camera. My voice cracked like a seventh grader's, and, at one point, I nearly deafened the soundman with the headphones by knocking the microphone off the table. Halfway through my five-minute retort the reporter pulled out a pack of cigarettes and began showing definite withdrawal symptoms. Two-thirds of the way through he leaned back and blew smoke rings of capitulation at the ceiling, or maybe at God. When I finally finished he threw his pencil in the air as people did with their hats on V-J Day. Meacham put a fatherly arm around my shoulder and ushered me out.

Over the next two days I never had the chance to test myself again. Not only was the press in St. Louis and Kansas City lacking hostility, but they were quite clearly sympathetic to the cause. It boosted my optimism for a successful October 15, but left a more important question unresolved.

Was the Vietnam Moratorium going to change anyone's mind about the war or the antiwar movement? The Moratorium was intended to be a two-pronged effort—first, mobilize those who were already against the war, and second, educate those who were not. The first was easy. It entailed no more than calling an already amenable person and asking him to be at a certain place at a certain time. The second, however, the arduous task of educating, of convincing those who disagree, placed doubts in my mind. Was I or any of the other young organizers around the country equipped with that kind of patience? The answer to that was still several months away, and I tried to push it from my mind. The trip, like the organizing before it, had gone well. For now that was enough. It was ten o'clock at night when my plane from Kansas City arrived at National Airport in Washington. I took a cab to 1029 Vermont Avenue.

The entire face of the office had changed. At the far end of the room some new secretary was standing at the Xerox machine, grinding out copies of a new press release, and next to her the robotype (typewriter that needs no typist) was chattering away, writing thank-you letters to contributors.

I dropped my bags and went into the middle office room where Dick and I and a map had gotten to know each other for three months. Dick wasn't there—still with the flying circus in Ohio. But the room wasn't empty; it was filled with several new staffers who were helping with the campus organizations. Of course it had to happen; the unwieldly areas with which Dick and I were working simply had to be subdivided and managed by additional staff, but just the same I selfishly felt a bit disheartened to see the quaintness of our small group become a thing of the past. I excused myself from these strangers, and went back out into the reception room to rest on the couch for a moment. As I sat there more new faces filtered in and out of the room. Many stopped where I was sitting and asked rather hurriedly whether I could be helped. I said I didn't think so.

Up until now, organizing the Moratorium had been an uphill effort. But in the life-cycle of every successful campaign there come a mysterious and imperceptible moment when the crest of the hill is reached and inertia turns from foe to ally. After that it's all moving under its own momentum, and the task of the original organizers becomes one of jogging, then running, then racing alongside it, giving it a helpful sideways nudge every so often to keep it on a true path. That moment for the Moratorium had been reached.

During this day and a half spent in Washington I was surrounded by an air of action and importance. People talked faster, sounded surer, and interacted with one another with more intensity than a month earlier. The mood was sometimes near manic. Mounting tension and hours of work could lead one moment's reel of nervous laughter into snapping tempers. Emotionally and physically spent, no one cared by the day's fifteenth hour of work to argue any more. "Then do what you want. I'm going to bed," became an integral part of the decision-making process.

Brown, however, always seemed to be the one person in the group able to cope with his tattered nerve endings and ironless blood without resorting to flagellation of bystanders. I suppose that's one of the reasons he's been such an effective organizer over the years. When things got tight he was more likely to begin pacing or tearing bits of paper into an empty coffee cup than raise his voice to anyone.

Coming out of his office and seeing me stretched out on the

couch, totally nonplussed by the changed atmosphere, Sam flashed an impudent smile and tossed a copy of *The New Republic* in my lap. I took it into his office to read it. Hawk waved hello from a phone, Marge blew me a motherly kiss, and Mixner stared out the window. I sat down and began reading. There on the cover was an editorial that heaped verbal bouquets upon the Moratorium, depicting October 15 as Easter, Yom Kippur, and Bastille Day all rolled into one.

"How do you like *that* for a shot in the arm?" Sam asked with a gloat and a gleam. "I couldn't have written that kind of praise better myself." He took the magazine back and placed it with special care atop his cleanest coffee mug. This was the kind of breakthrough he had been waiting for. Never was there doubt in his mind that the student participation in the Moratorium would be enormous. The greater question had been whether or not a large part of the adult community could be induced to join. Now, with a cover endorsement from the Bible of the liberal-wing Democrats, it was nearly assured that most of the old McCarthy and Kennedy voters would take part in the protest. This delighted Brown. No matter how flirtatious he may get with the student left, he has always known that the game is won or lost in the suburban living rooms of doctors and lawyers and businessmen across the country. Because of that pervasive sense of the practical, Brown has always played to a more moderate crowd than almost any major antiwar leader. His way seemed to be working where others (more militant and sectarian) hadn't, and I found myself all for it.

Sam, Hawk, Mixner, and Marge continued their discussion that had been begun before I had come into the office. They were debating whom to ask for endorsements to be put in a full-page ad in the Sunday *New York Times*. I meandered around the room, noting whatever other news I needed to catch up on. Atop Sam's desk was a note from Lawrence Spivak inviting Brown to appear on "Meet the Press," and tacked up on the wall was a front-page article from yesterday's *New York Times* that had been garnished by Hawk's red felt pen. I went right to the underlined parts. "The Nixon Administration," it said, "is considering a series of major reforms in the military draft to defuse domestic political opposition to the war in Vietnam." It continued, "He [an 'outside source'] contended that his report was plausible because several antiwar groups [*sic.*] were planning to call for a moratorium in the classrooms across the country in the form of a national strike on October 15. The President, the source said, is aware of this movement and will try to take the steam out of it with the draft reform and troop withdrawals."

What a boff! A month away, and already October 15 was meaning something to the power swingers. It filled me at once with a conceited pride in our group, and more nobly with a rejuvenated faith in the possibility of average people affecting the course of political events. Things had already gone certainly beyond *my* expectations. When I had joined the Moratorium in May it was perhaps mostly to fulfill a personal need, not especially because I thought I could actually help change anything. I had wanted to be actively against the war if only to de-escalate the conflict within my own mind. Even if the project had ended a failure, it still would have been a personal triumph, just oozing with existential worth. But now the dimensions had changed, and thus my attitude had changed as well. Now it seemed that the Moratorium might very well be effective, and therefore it simply *had* to be effective. I could accept history as anything but a tease. For the first time I felt that it was no longer merely a personal commitment against the war, but that I was part of a movement that would either win or lose. We were here and they were there. We had our maps and strategy, and somewhere in the deepest corridors of the White House and Pentagon they had theirs. For five years the war makers had been winning. For five years they had been turning the Vietnam landscape into blood and vomit, and had been winning the allegiance of an American majority. After five years of war the biggest showdown was yet to come. We were going to say no, god damn it, and we were going to be heard.

My last desire in the world was to leave the Washington office before the hour of that showdown, but my last year of college and its 2S deferment beckoned. I took the next afternoon's flight for Boston. It was two-thirty when I got to Leverett House.

I pushed open the door to my new seventh-floor room and slid my bags in along the naked linoleum floor ahead of me. The grey cinderblock walls were bare, and so was the blue-striped mattress and black metal frame in the corner. Dust had been collecting atop the vacant dresser and in the empty bookshelves. In the center of the room was a black wooden chair with copper-colored armrests and the Harvard inscription of "Ve Ri Tas" on the back. Hiding between its legs on the floor was a short-corded black phone. The afternoon sun over the Charles River was beating down through the smudged picture window, heating the room unbearably.

After I opened the side windows and jammed some old magazines under the door to keep the breeze from slamming it shut, I took the phone in my lap and dialed Davis Hall at Wellesley College.

"Marcie?"

"Kenny?"

I sighed, then she sighed, then I sighed again. Together we sounded like a slow leak.

"I'm at Leverett House, honey. Why don't you come in?"

"Beg me."

"Arf, arf!"

"I'll be there in half an hour." *Click*.

For the next thirty minutes I sat in the straight-back chair, staring at the pockmarked cinderblocks, thinking how beautiful a simple decor can look some days. Then Marcie appeared in the doorway. She dropped her purse and we fell into each other's arms and lives again. I stumbled back upon the mattress, pulling Marcie on top of me, letting her long, honey-colored hair fall across my face. The sleeves of her sweater were rolled up and the skin on her arms and face smelled of fresh outdoors. I stroked the small of her back as we lay there cooing like a couple of school kids, which in fact is what we were. After about ten minutes of kissing we said, "Hi."

I heard someone knock on the open door and say, " Hello in there." It was Cheyney Ryan, my roommate since freshman year. Without lifting my head I took one of my hands from Marcie's back and waved.

"As long as you two aren't doing anything, how 'bout throwing a ball around down at the river?"

With my hand still raised, I lowered all but my middle finger. Cheyney said he'd see us later. I rolled Marcie over and away from me so I could get up and close the door. On the way back the nagging bitch on the floor began ringing. "Nag, nag, nag." I let it ring three times and picked up the receiver. It was Ray Dougan, the fellow who Marge had told me ran the Mass. PAX office over on Brattle Street. I was to use that office for New England organizing.

"Yes, Ray . . . right, I'm sorry I didn't have a chance to get in touch with you. Uh, huh . . . well . . ." I looked at Marcie apologetically. "Yeah, ten minutes is fine." I hung up and explained to Marcie I had to go over to the Cambridge office to meet Ray and go with him to an organizational meeting for high-school students at B.U. She said she had brought some of her philosophy books along, and that that would be fine. We could talk later. I kissed her again and left.

It was about a five-minute walk over to the office at 44 Brattle Street in Harvard Square. The building was a quaint

New England gray wooden structure squeezed among Cambridge's chic clothing shops. In between all the satin-sleeved and bell-bottomed manikins there hung from our third-floor window a thirty-foot banner reading, "Work for Peace." Rumor had it one of the manikins next door was a government agent.

I went in the main entrance and up the narrow stairway. As I turned the corner on the second floor landing I was met head on by this bearded fellow who was staggering down the steps having trouble seeing over the box he was carrying. Not seeing me he lurched forward and with a grunt I was pinned against the wall.

"Is someone there?" the fellow asked from the other side of the gigantic cardboard container.

"I yield!" I gasped, trying to bring my hands up between the box and my chest.

"Give me a hand, will you?" he said.

"Take a step back," I answered, "and I'll do anything you want."

He stumbled one step backward, I grabbed the edge that had accosted my rib cage, and together we took the load down to the sidewalk in front. My new playmate turned out to be Ray Dougan. The box we carried was full of Moratorium literature.

"Come on," he said after we introduced ourselves. "Let's get this into the car and over to B.U." We loaded the box into his rickety maroon station wagon and chugged on away for the meeting. Ray was a law student at Boston University, but his work with the Moratorium left him time for maybe one class every couple of weeks. He was an irresistibly likeable fellow. His manner was much like Brown's, soft-spoken, easy sell, an ameliorator of office arguments. But unlike Brown, Ray didn't seem to have the underlying political drive and ambition. Dougan was more in the American Friends' Service Committee mold, no doctrinaire view of all world politics, only an intuitive sickening at the thought of men training other men to kill yet other men. He was deferred from the draft because he was the only son in the family and his father had been killed in World War II.

The banged-up auto puttered and wheezed down Storrow Drive in third as though it were still in first, while Ray and I discussed plans for a Boston rally.

"The only thing I know for sure," I said, "is that McGovern is willing to give a speech, but his staffers want it to be in a small indoor place so they can soak up all that overflow crowd publicity." Ray looked at me with a grin as if to say, "Bless their little election-minded hearts."

"Well, actually," he said after thinking for a moment, "that's all right. I think if there's going to be a rally it *should* be small so we can concentrate on the community canvassing." Ray was a grass-roots man from way back. Extravaganzas repulsed him. "We should try to have the plans for that firmed up in the next day or so." I nodded my agreement and looked out the car window at the sailboats on the river. As each rounded the far bouy to head downwind, a new red or yellow or blue striped spinnaker unfolded in the afternoon sun. The stiff autumn blows pushed the boats fast enough to cut white water around their bows. Next fall, I thought, I would make time to take up sailing.

We stayed at the meeting only long enough to distribute our literature and for me to give a couple of minutes' speech to the hundred or so high-school coordinators that had come. Not inspired rhetoric—it would have met stiff competition at any Eagle's Club testimonial. I thought about Marcie during most of it. But the students there didn't really need any pep talk; they were ready to go. They sat with their red-fisted T-shirts and Resistance buttons, leaning over the fronts of their seats, waiting to sign up their orders for antiwar materials so they could get back to their neighborhoods and begin working. When I was in high school the only thing we tried to organize was "school spirit." Political awareness has cascaded well down the age brackets since then. These students saw themselves as a political force, a thought that had never seriously occurred to any of *us* four years earlier.

On the drive back to Cambridge, Ray took his hand from the rattling gear shift and put it in a fist on the rattling dashboard. "That's where it's at, man," he said. "In the high schools. The political consciousness those kids take with them to college is going to determine this country's history in the '70s and '80s." He put his hand back on the stick and rammed it back into second as he slowed the car for the Harvard Square exit. "Yep," he agreed with himself, "even the non-activist youth culture types, the ones who at least have the right instincts—they're going to be the new silent majority." I agreed too, and thought back with a kinder spirit on Atlantic City. "No, man, politics just isn't where my head's at." That's what the fellow there had said to me. A better silent majority, that's what he would hopefully become.

When we got back to the Brattle Street office I was introduced to Jeff, a Harvard sophomore, who had been working for the past couple of weeks at organizing the Boston-area campuses. He threw his head to the side, snapping all of his fashionably long blond hair in place, and grasped my hand with a political sureness that belied his age. His speech was wrapped in an impenetrable layer of New York prep. He flicked the ashes from his Tiparillo into a gray metal wastebasket and said, "Let's talk." He led me into one of the office's back rooms and closed the door behind us. Throwing his head to the side again he settled into the large green vinyl chair next to the window and propped his feet upon the radiator. "You know what's been happening here over the last week?" he asked. I shook my head no. "Good, then I'll tell you." He put the plastic tip of the cigar between his teeth and began telling me.

He told me that the student body president from Boston

College (whom, apparently, Lavine had contacted over the summer) had called an all-Boston campus meeting for the following
night to decide on a Boston rally. He had sent invitations to all
the student government and newspaper people we had been in
touch with from the Washington office, but had specified that
the meeting would be open to everyone else as well. In the
meantime Jeff had learned that the members of the Student
Mobilization Committee were planning on packing that meeting. This is one of the most basic tactics used by movement
groups, seeing who can get the greatest number of people to an
organizational meeting, even if that number is disproportionate
to the people they actually represent. Because the groups that
are farthest left are almost by definition the most activist, they
generally fare the best in this department. Jeff gnawed nervously
at his cigar like a big-time city boss. I saw the problem.

The Student Mobilization Committee (or SMC or Student
Mobe, a distinct organization from the New Mobe) leaders are
also the leaders of the Young Socialists' Alliance (YSA). The
YSA, in turn, is the student version of the Socialist Workers'
Party, the main Trotskyite group in this country. Thus, the
Student Mobe leaders are known in the antiwar movement as
the "Trots" or, as Sam and Marge called them, "the weirdo
Trots." The SMC'ers, however, never admit to the connection.
One Student Mobe leader was quoted in the *Boston Globe* as
saying, "Oh, yes, wasn't Trotsky some Russian in the '20s?"
Hmm!

Whereas the Moratorium Committee never had a general
ideology but only sought to gather as many people as possible
around the single issue of immediate withdrawal from Vietnam,
the SMC Trots were clearly after a socialist revolution. The
Trotskyite strategy is essentially this: form alliances with anyone (liberals, conservatives, vegetarians, *anyone*) who is willing
to go into the streets or to a rally because of some particular issue; it is then hoped that once those people *do* go to rallies and

listen to enough Trot speakers, they will come to see the larger "contradictions" in a capitalistic society. The single issue, in other words, is the vehicle to a pervasive class consciousness. Needless to say, we and they had rather different rally speakers in mind.

Our main fear was that if the rally were controlled by the most radical segment of the antiwar movement, then either the greater numbers of moderates wouldn't show up, or if they did, that after enough revolutionary rhetoric, the rally would end early in anger and disunity. Either way the Moratorium would have failed to bring new masses actively into the antiwar movement, and most importantly, it would have failed to show Nixon that his opposition was united. "Whatever we do," I had told the high schoolers that afternoon, "we want to unite, not split, the antiwar movement." It was becoming clear that I may as well have told them to twine and bind the San Andreas Fault.

"Any suggestions?" I asked Jeff when he finished his woeful tale. He dropped the butt of his Tiparillo into a half-filled coffee cup. It hissed as it hit the cold, day-old brew and emitted the pungent fumes of a dead cigar.

"No, but I suggest we come up with something by tomorrow night's meeting."

"Yeah, well, let's sleep on it tonight. I'll give you a call tomorrow."

When I got back to Leverett House it was nearly seven o'clock. I walked catatonically through the dinner line, totally absorbed by the thoughts of the new dilemma. I almost forgot to steal a dinner for Marcie. We sat at a small table in the far corner of the spacious dining room. Except for a few lingering students and the white-aproned women who wash the tables, the place was empty. My stomach was getting nervous and upset, and I thought everyone left in the hall could hear it gurgle. While Marcie ate and told me about Italy, I picked away at my food like an archeologist, turning the breaded veal over and over again, trying to find a crisp spot somewhere. I nodded at everything she said and laughed in all the wrong places.

"All right, what's wrong?" she wanted to know.

"Well . . ." I paused to cut off the greasiest part of the veal and drop it into my glass of milk to see if it looked as disgusting as I thought it would. It did and I smiled.

"I don't know, maybe I'm just not cut out for this kind of organizing. I've always got to be working *against* someone, always got to think about out-maneuvering someone; and I get all tight inside."

Marcie took my hand in hers and pressed it against her cheek. "I know," I said, "we'll pack our bags tonight and move to the Virgin Islands, and make love until we're eighty." She smiled, but it was a troubled smile.

"No, I don't really want to leave either," I said. "Come on." We got up from the table and walked arm in arm back to my room.

The next night an early autumn drizzle had Cambridge and Boston in a misty slick. Seven of us crammed and lap-seated ourselves into Jeff's GTO to drive over to Boston College. That whole afternoon we had sat around the office, drumming our fingers on our foreheads, failing to devise an acceptable way of preventing a radical takeover at the meeting. The only new information was that the student-body president from B.C. had called and asked that I speak first and said that he would then chair the rest of the discussion. The trip over was the last opportunity for us Moratorium people to map our strategy.

"This is the way I see it," Jeff began as he lit up a Tiparillo. "If we don't use their kind of tactics we're going to get massacred." He blew the smoke out his window and rolled through a stop sign that he claimed was optional. "And there are only so many ways we can make sure this meeting comes out right. All we have to do is think of one of them."

"I don't see why anything has to even be put to a vote to-night," someone next to me in the back seat said. "Just outline what the plans for the fifteenth are and tell them we all gotta start working right away." Sometimes elitist simplicity is very appealing, especially when it holds promise of a short meeting.

"No, no, no," Jeff objected from up front. "Too heavy-handed. Way too heavy." His foot pressed down on the accelerator as he negotiated the next corner into total surrender. "What we have to do is make like everything is up in the air and that we have to wait a day or two before we can decide anything." The minds were really clicking now as my stomach began knotting like dried-out hemp. "Then we hold a second meeting later tonight back in Ken's room and release our plans to the press for the next morning." But of course! No need for baroque tales and complex schemes. Just one simple, straight-forward act of deceit. Who could be offended? . . . Well, at least, who of those offended could do anything about it? That would teach them to pack our meetings. It was a clear case of Do Unto Others Before They Do Unto You. With peace in our hearts and fraud on our lips we entered the meeting.

It was being held in a small science lecture room. At the front was a table and blackboard (post-1950 green type). Tiers of semicircled seats extended to the back wall. The flourescent lights and linoleum floor made one think (as I'm sure the architect intended) of ions and gamma rays, not of rallies and marches. We were a little late, and most of the people to come to this meeting had already settled in for a long, hard evening. Some were resting their elbows on the writing boards that pull up from the sides of the seats. Of the sixty or so to attend only two were over 30, but with that number I could extend my limits of trust.

I let my eyes ramble up and down the rows of seats, look-ing for the radical contingent, the Trots, whom I expected to come with fatigues showing below their jeans and ammo belts bulging beneath their work shirts. Nothing of that sort was evident, though, and so I fell back upon my second method of calculation. Look for all the people with wire-rimmed glasses who are taking four and five second drags on their filterless cigarettes (Lucky Strike and Pall Mall would be out of business without radicals) and then letting the smoke seep from their noses or come out spasmodically through their mouths as they talked. Liberals generally jet the smoke out their mouths, because that's the way the models on television do it to create springtime. Mine was a scientific method of political pigeon-holing, but my calculations were quickly interrupted.

"Let's get on with it!" someone said loudly. "We hardly have enough time to plan for October 15 as it is." Mumbles of unanimous agreement. That pretty well castrated the "we have to wait a couple days" plan. These people weren't about to wait for anything. I looked at Jeff, whose shrugging shoulders silently advised, "If you punt, face the other way, please."

There was no rap of a gavel, only a signal from the B.C. student president for me to come up and begin talking. I walked calmly to the front (as only men pretending they still have a plan can walk) and rather than taking the chair behind the table, instead opted to sit on the table's front corner. It was a derivation of the method used by young sociology and psychology teachers who on the first day of class take off their shoes and sit cross-legged atop their desks just to show they're one of the gang.

There they were, the waiting faces of the disparate American Left. What the hell, give reasoning a whirl. I tugged nervously at my collar and began. I said that when we planned our rally we shouldn't try to fuse eight or nine differing positions or issues that will tend to split the group but should instead pick the one issue or position that is the common denominator. Everyone in the antiwar movement has a differing position on civil rights, women's lib, socialism. The only genuine point of agreement is the demand for U.S. withdrawal from Vietnam. Therefore, any rally speaker should address himself only to that view that everyone holds in common. Someone like—oh, say George McGovern.

At the utterance of the name half the group smiled and nodded. The other half sat stoically, letting the smoke from their filterless cigarettes seep from their noses and curl around their wire-rimmed glasses. I was right! There was a whole battalion of them scattered strategically around the room.

"It seems, though, that any rally we have," I said, playing to the newly identified allies, "should be small enough to not detract from community canvassing that day." The first hand went up. It was from one of the SMC'ers I had met at the B.U. meeting the day before. At that time he told me I was foolish if I thought any antiwar movement could exist without the far left. But at that time our disagreement was purely academic. The raised hand was the first I had seen of him this night.

"Who else would you plan on having speak beside liberal politicians?" he asked with an edge of smoke wrapped about each word. *Liberal politician* amid the student far left is somewhat comparable to *gook*, *Jap*, and *Kraut* in American trenches.

"Well, I don't say it *has* to be a liberal politician. I just think it should be someone who will stick to the subject of Vietnam. After all, we're trying to *include*, not alienate, the businessmen and housewives who are willing to stand on immediate withdrawal." Ten more hands shot up from all around the room. Now I could be selective about which attackers I called on.

"It seems to me," a girl with a T-shirt and short brown hair began, "that a lot of people are going to be angry if there aren't any speakers with a little more radical analysis of the war than George McGovern."

Before I could answer another fellow got up from the rear Trots gallery (a group that huddled together between questions). "Why are you against having more radical speakers? Don't you believe in free speech?" They must have concurred in that little huddle that I was a diehard liberal who could be floored with one good jab to the free-speech tendon. I looked over to my compatriots. Why weren't *they* huddling for the answers?

"Well—I'm not *really* against radical speakers per se." (I would first have to get my foot out of my mouth before I could lie through my teeth.) "I'm only concerned about the greatest amount of appeal of the rally, and I don't want to see community people continue to be turned off by the antiwar movement." No one could fault *that* statement. Now was the moment for humility. "But these are only my personal views. The exact nature of any rallies we hold in Boston *should* be determined by a group like this." The Trots that had indeed flooded the meeting kept right on, first from one side of the room, then the other. I answered the attacks with a surprising amount of cool, but silently I was wishing I were nine years old so I could just start screaming, "Weirdo Trots, weirdo Trots!" and run out of the room bawling.

Finally someone from my team got to his feet. It was Jeff (without his Tiparillo). "What Ken is trying to say is that our Moratorium office in Cambridge isn't a decision-making center." His outstretched arms reeked of innocence. "We're only there to help coordinate all the activities planned around Massachusetts." There's the word, "coordinate"—a fine polysyllabic word used by every political organizer who doesn't want to admit he's making all the decisions. After October 15 Brown used to pay periodic visits to our Massachusetts Moratorium office to discuss future months' Moratorium activities. Sam was exceptionally good at using the word. He would always preface the discussion with, "I'm not here to bring information *from* Washington but to *take* information back with me. Our only purpose down there is to *coordinate* the activities you local offices have decided on." And we would all smile, knowing that two days later we would read in the papers that the Washington office had announced the actions that the local Moratorium organizations were to undertake for the following month. It was a friendly enough game. Brown played it with us and we played it with the local communities in New England. Everyone knew the rules and knew that no one made decisions, but only "coordinated" activities.

"In that case"—my Trot friend from B.U. had recaptured the floor—"the best thing would be for you to hold the small McGovern rally that you want, and those of us who want a mass rally will have one someplace else." Everyone agreed. Only after the meeting did the moderates we talked to realize what they had been agreeing to.

"That sounds fine," I said with bedridden enthusiasm. "Let's get on with the meeting." The Boston College president took over and I slinked back to my seat with the diminished sprightliness of one who had scored three points in the first round but had given up twenty-four. The discussion that followed concerned the mass rally. All agreed that the sprawling Boston Common would be the ideal location. The park permit for October 15 had been taken out in midsummer by a Northeastern University student who had been in touch with our office in Washington. That priceless shard of paper in his pocket made him the most flattered and wooed student in all of Boston. He leaned back in his seat throughout the meeting, his arms spread wide across the backs of the seats next to him, enjoying the extra politeness he received whenever he spoke.

Once the generalities of the rally were dispensed with, the meeting went the way of all organizational meetings—that is, as all flesh turns to dust, all meetings turn to committee assignments. It's part of the cosmic order. Finance Committee, Publicity Committee, and of course the Speakers' Committee. Each subgroup contained approximately half of us and half of them.

We had all read George Kennan on balance of power. By nine-thirty all the committee meetings had been arranged and this first organizational meeting was adjourned. Handshakes and pleasantries all the way out the door, each side knowing that the other would return to its home base for more private attempts to gain control of the Boston rally.

Thus far, the SMC had proved the better competitor, rising in one short, meeting-packing evening from no voice at all to half a say in the October plans. It made me wonder just how many of these political maneuverings were going on in cities around the country that the Washington Moratorium office didn't know about. From that central headquarters it was virtually impossible to determine the actual nature of what was being planned at the other end of the telephone wire. In antiwar organizing, like everything else, control is inversely proportional to distance. And for all the idealism that may shuttle one into antiwar organizing, it's still a part of politics, and control is the ballgame. My innocence was falling out in clumps and shocks.

As the several dozen people echoed down the empty hallway toward the front door, I slipped into one of the building's alcoves, where I found several public telephones. They weren't installed in booths, just wall mountings. Two were being used by people who I didn't think had been at the meeting. I took the third and called collect to Washington.

"Sam? How's it goin'? . . . Good. Listen, the reason I'm calling is . . . well, things aren't happening in Boston quite the way I thought they were." I then proceeded to explain that there was going to be a mass rally whether we liked it or not and that if we didn't help organize it the SMC would do it all. "It could be a disaster!" I squawked. The strangers next to me looked over and I lowered my voice. "I mean if we can't get the moderates to show up, it's just going to be the usual small rally, and whether we had anything to do with it or not, the press is going to attribute it to us. Let's face it, anything happening on October 15 is going to be called Moratorium." There was a long pause and a sigh from the other end.

"So you want McGovern to be at the rally."

"Well, yeah. And if you can get him quick we can just announce our plans to the press and forget about this whole meeting tonight." Politics had me where it wanted me.

"Yeah, all right, Ken, I'll try to get him. What time on the 15?"

"Three-thirty. That's the time everyone here tonight thought would be best."

"Ok, just don't panic and I'll try to get McGovern to show for an outdoor rally. Give me a call tomorrow night."

I hung up and walked briskly down the abandoned corridor toward the front of the building. Pushing through the glass doors, I came out onto the wet pavement and took a deep breath of the cool, damp air. The drizzle had stopped some time during the meeting, but the streets still glistened with the white of headlights and red of taillights. Somewhere in the distance was a siren, but that was blocks and lives away. My mind had room for only one thing, keeping political control of the Boston Common rally. Jesus, did I have a stomach ache!

Over the next day and a half, we made all our own arrangements for the rally—obtained McGovern for the main speech, okayed everything with the Boston Common permit holder, had people to handle the rally logistics, et cetera, et cetera, ho-hum, et cetera. That afternoon we would announce our plans to the *Boston Globe* for the following morning's papers.

But then . . . the *call!* It was Jeff. "Ken, I just came from Galbraith's Office. Thought maybe ol' JKG would want to be the emcee, and guess what. He had just called McGovern to tell him *not* to give a speech in an open park. Has to be in a stadium."

"Oh, for Christ's sake, why?!"

"I don't know, but he told him that the Boston Common is a bad place to speak."

"So we're right back with our own private McGovern rally to compete with a mass Boston Common rally, right?"

"Yep, a real ball-buster, huh."

"Yeah, well, thanks for the news. Talk to you later." *Click.* 202/347-4757.

"Paula, this is Ken. Sam free?" Two minutes of silent payment to Bell Telephone.

Then, "Yeah, Ken. What's up?"

"I just heard Galbraith advised McGovern to stay away from the Common."

"Yeah, I just talked to him."

"I suppose he just *happens* to want him in Harvard Stadium." Some Harvard professors have a tendency to think that all the stars and galaxies were catapulted into the heavens from Cambridge, Massachusetts. If they only knew how Harvard-MIT arrogance made Cambridge an anathema to the rest of Boston activists.

"No, he says any stadium is OK. Anyplace where there's more control of the stage and mikes than in the park."

"Like Harvard Stadium."

"No, any stadium."

"Harvard Stadium."

"Damn it, Ken. I just *talked* to him." Good Lord, I had actually run to the end of Mr. Brown's patience.

Contritely, "OK, OK—didn't mean to be edgy with *you*—is there anything you can do to get McGovern back on the Common? We were going to announce the rally plans today. You know, another day or so and that SMC-packed speakers' committee will meet and announce their own plans."

"I'd like to help but I can't. Galbraith simply carries more weight with McGovern than me." Pause—"shit"—pause. "You're going to have to convince Galbraith."

"Yeah, OK Sam. Thanks anyway. I'll see what we can do."
There was no doubt about it, I couldn't call JKG himself. I had
never met him, and I never speak to people over 6 feet 7 anyway.
Like many political problems, I took it to my tutor and friend,
Marty Peretz. Aside from being a key financial backer of the
Moratorium, I thought maybe on the grounds of pure knowl-
edgability he might hold some sway with Galbraith. Asking
Peretz to ask Galbraith to ask McGovern. Press the button that
tips the lever that moves the rod that turns the spindle that
cranks the wheel. Such is the world of organizing.

Eventually McGovern was scheduled back on the Common.
But the delay was irreparable. By the time Marty was able to
reach Galbraith and Galbraith was able to reach McGovern
three days had passed, the speakers' committee had met twice
and announced its plans and, as the saying goes, the Lady had
been robbed of her do-hicky. The entire public had been in-
formed that McGovern would be the main speaker but that
the second in line would be the SMC's choice, Peter Camejo,
Socialist Workers' Party candidate for the Senate in Massachusetts. Almost all of us in the Cambridge Moratorium office continued to be upset about the two speaking together. All of us,
that is, except Ray.

"I'm sorry we've gotten into this whole thing," Ray said
with disgust late one night. He rubbed his eyes and took a sip
of hot tea from his mug. "I was hoping the Moratorium would
be more than just another rally organization. This whole Boston
Common extravaganza is going to totally upstage the community canvassing." He buttoned his red and black lumberjacket
and turned to close the window on the chilly night air. "But
that's not even the worst part of what's been happening. As
long as we're stuck with putting on a rally, let's not spend
twenty-four hours a day fighting other antiwar groups. They're
not the enemy. We're putting this thing on *with* the SMC and
that's that. It's not going to be such a disaster to have someone

more radical than George McGovern up there. I'm tired of the
mutual deceit that's been going on. We and they are just going
to have to sit down and start accommodating each other more."
He rested his folded hands across the mod tie that had flopped
outside of his lumberjacket and tilted his head back to the edge
of the chair. "I don't know . . . I just think it's time we gain
a little perspective."

He was of course right. To be sure, the Trots were willing
to work with "liberals" only because they drew bigger crowds
that would then also listen to their own more radical speakers,
and as Camejo himself said, "We want liberal speakers on the
same platform with us so the people can clearly see who are
the phonies." But the fact remained that they *were*, unlike
farther-left groups like SDS, willing to form wider coalitions
in order to end the war. They were neither as sectarian nor as
morally purist as SDS.

And so, despite some continued tensions and anxieties,
the two groups *did* learn to live with each other. An uneasy
coalition, but a coalition just the same. The mechanics of organizing the rally and the door-to-door canvassing were in
motion, and I withdrew from the Boston scene to continue organizing in the other New England states. In places like Vermont
and New Hampshire and Maine there were no battles with the
left. The only battle there was to get people moving left *enough*
on the war issue to take *some* type of action on October 15.
There one had to surmount the hostility from the right, but
after two weeks of antiwar group infighting in Boston, the shift
to a more conservative area wasn't totally without relief.

But if I had escaped the heat treatment of the left at
work, I certainly had no such fortune at home. There I was outflanked by roommates who viewed me as everything from the
"resident liberal" to "still a helluva nice dupe." Early in the
fall, while I was spending most of my time on the room phone

talking to Moratorium campus coordinators, my roommate Cheyney was busy getting elected head of Harvard's SDS as as well as co-editor of SDS's national paper, *New Left Notes*. I eventually began closing my bedroom door when I used the phone. When we were alone together we tried to stay off of politics, but that generally left us in very silent rooms. In years past we had been able to go on for hours about a million and seven shared interests—we had even written a full-length musical comedy together. But that was all past. Every day now our lives were being more and more narrowly defined by our politics, his even more than mine, as radical politics is far more consuming than any other brand. He didn't want to write any more musical comedies—they were "bourgeois" and "irrelevant."

During the first week of October a friend of mine from the University of Wisconsin called long distance and asked incredulously, "My God, are you and Cheyney still living together?"

"Yeah, sure, why?"

"Take a look at the latest issue of *New Left Notes* . . . oh, and Ken, remember homocide is ten years minimum."

It was nearly midnight as I hung up and raced down to the newsstand to pick up a copy. All out. Over to the Moratorium office—they subscribed (liberal open-mindedness and all that crap). I found my friend John Gage, the rally logistics expert, sitting at the receptionist's desk with the latest issue in his lap. He shook his head and chortled, "You two keep living together and one of you is going to get bounced as an organization fink." I snatched the paper away.

Front page editorial headline: "Moratorium is a Cover, Not a Solution." The byline belonged to Cheyney and two others. I read on. "In fact, we think that though there are many honest people involved in the Moratorium, the basic aim of the Moratorium leadership is to destroy the antiwar movement." And I had just lent him my Tom Rush album, too! The article got even better as I continued reading. The Moratorium leaders were "liars" and the whole protest was a part of the war mongers' "strategy."

So much for "let's stay off of politics!" Ten minutes later I was back at Leverett House sitting in the living room rocking chair with the paper on my lap, like a father waiting up at night with his son's report card. Quarter till one, in walked Cheyney.

" 'Lo."

"Hi 'ya schmuckhead. You're just the revolutionary I wanted to see."

He walked to the opposite side of the room and settled his large frame into one of the desk chairs for a possibly long encampment. "All right, let's hear it. What in the article don't you think is true?"

"Oh, let's take 'out to destroy the antiwar movement' for starters. I'd call that a little verbal overkill, wouldn't you?"

Cheyney cupped his hands behind his neck and arched his back in the confining wooden chair for a little arguing room. "Well, I have to admit that that's the one statement I disagreed with, but I was outvoted by the other two writers." I remained expressionless and unmoved. "No, that's true," he insisted. "I would have preferred a phrase like 'whether unwittingly or not.' " All right, so much for that point. We had more to discuss. And we discussed it, 'round and 'round for the next three and a half hours.

He would throw up his hands in frustration and ask for a sixth time, "How can you ally with the congressmen and capitalist bosses who are responsible for the war?! Bringing people back to the fold of the Democratic Party, that's all the Moratorium is doing. You're giving it the legitimacy it needs when it engineers the next war."

I would grip the curved armrests and push the rocking

chair backward to reply for a seventh time, "Damn it, Cheyney, you want to end the war, and still you do everything you can to exclude people from the antiwar movement. You think this country should be communist? Fine. Convince me *after* we end the war, which may just happen if you people would stop being so piss-ass self-righteous and stop thinking everyone else in the world is a pig." My voice was trembling. We had been together for over three years and I felt a special closeness, a special need to make him see. But there seemed to be no purpose in arguing. Our assumptions and goals were simply too divergent. I was fighting militarism, he was fighting capitalists. He believed the two were synonymous. I didn't. By the time dawn blinked and stretched, we were both fighting off sleep. He went to his bed wondering why I didn't see that until the revolution comes things would always be the same. I went to my bed wondering why he didn't see that as long as people continue thinking in terms of revolution and war things would always be the same. We're both out of school now—I graduated and he was ex- pelled for one too many SDS occupation—and every time we see each other I sense we're both still wondering.

During those first two weeks of October the outpouring of antiwar sentiment throughout the country was incredible. The Moratorium had become the rallying point. Millions of quiet dissenters had reached their "protest threshold" and were now ready to join the students. Every morning I would thumb through the *Boston Globe* and find article after article about this new phenomenon called the Moratorium. BIPARTISAN GROUP OF SENATORS AND REPRESENTATIVES BACK MORATORIUM; SEVENTY- NINE COLLEGE PRESIDENTS SEND LETTER TO NIXON URGING QUICK WITHDRAWAL; REPRESENTATIVES TO TRY TO KEEP CONGRESS IN SESSION ALL NIGHT ON OCTOBER 14TH; GOODELL INTRODUCES A BILL WITH DECEMBER 1, 1970, WITHDRAWAL DEADLINE; COLLEGE ADMINISTRATIONS ANNOUNCE OPTIONAL CLASSES AND IN DOZENS

OF CASES COMPLETE CLOSING FOR THE 15TH; REUTHER (UAW)
FITZGIBBONS (TEAMSTERS) AND BOYLE (INTERNATIONAL CHEM-
ICAL WORKERS) ENDORSE MORATORIUM; CITY COUNCILS AROUND
THE COUNTRY PASS ANTIWAR RESOLUTIONS; GROUPS OF DOCTORS
AND LAWYERS FILL NEWSPAPERS WITH ANTIWAR ADS.

There was a new national mood, and it seemed Nixon could
do nothing to assuage it. The Harris Poll showed the popular-
ity of Nixon's Vietnam policy down twelve percent since June
to an all-time low of thirty-seven percent. The thirty-five thousand troop withdrawal and autumn draft cuts had appeased no
one. At a press conference the president said of the protests,
"Under no circumstances will I be affected whatever by it."
That backfired nicely. Even his friends termed it a "callous,
ill-timed" statement for a president to make. Then it was to
the offensive. Secretary Rogers stated on national television
that the new wave of dissent made an early negotiation impossible. The ol' guilt ploy. Nixon wrote in an open letter to
a Georgetown University sophomore that this type of protest
would allow every group to test its strength "through confrontation in the streets." The ol' scare ploy. Agnew waved before
the American people a letter of endorsement the Moratorium
office had received from the leaders in Hanoi. Just plain ploy.
But it was all wasted energy. Nothing they said or did could
discredit the Moratorium or change people's plans to join the
protest on October 15. The Moratorium just kept growing, and
the whole world watched it grow.

My personal life changed in one very discernible way. It
disappeared. Every hour was consumed with thoughts and plans
for that coming Wednesday, that ides of October. I would
come home from the Brattle Street office, and just as Marcie
and I would be in each other's arms the phone would ring.
Marcie would wrap her arms around my ankles and scream,
"It's not for you!" There was always a panicked voice at the
other end. Some state coordinator in Vermont had sent a

CBS film crew to the wrong campus, or some congressman had been scheduled to speak in five different places at the same time. Always something that had to be rectified "right away."

And it seemed that overnight all of us organizing had become celebrities. What pure ego it was hunting through the papers and magazines for our pictures and quotes. I sent one picture of Ray, Jeff, and me in *Time* home to my parents. They said it was nice but asked, "Since when did you start smoking?" Comes with the job, Mom, no kidding. Even my teachers were reading about my political exploits. At the bottom of one of my Fine Arts 13 papers the section leader wrote, "Good luck with the Moratorium. I greatly admire your political work—pity you know nothing about art."

Schoolwork ignored, personal life usurped, image of self-importance bursting—thus did the first fourteen days of October pass. And finally, finally, finally came that last day BEFORE. It was the eve of October 14 as I scurried through dinner, spilling more than I ate. With milk stains above my lip I headed for the office, popping cookies in my mouth as I went. Marcie, as lovably apolitical as the day I met her, waited in my room studying her philosophy and drama. I walked through the Square, getting new charges of excitement as I passed all the store windows with signs stating their early closing hours on the 15. That's what we had said—if you can't shut down, close early. As long as everyone does what he feels he can afford to do. Outside the Brattle Theater was a group of students waiting to get into a Bogie flick. They were talking about getting up at six to canvass factories. Half a dozen townies were leaning against parked cars nearby. From a transistor radio came a rock DJ's voice, "Gettin' it together—only five more hours to M-day!" My adrenalin was on the climb.

Bounding up the stairs to our office I passed a middle-aged banker type bounding just as hurriedly *down* the stairs. On the lapel of his three-piece suit was our little blue and white dove button. Under his arm he was carrying a dozen "Work for Peace" posters. We smiled and said, "Hi." For the next twenty-four hours we would be the same age. I followed the clamor of voices and thunder of footsteps to the third floor.

At the top I just stood still for a moment, gazing at the Grand Central Station that had once been our five-room office suite. Hundreds of people, arguing, laughing, shouting, people were wending their way from room to room, all trying to be helpful but only adding to the general confusion. Eight more people were coming up the stairs behind me. The wall of flesh before me looked impenetrable, but I jumped in just the same. Poor Alwina, the receptionist, was trying to copy down a message from someone on the phone while a woman of about forty was *kvetching* in her other ear. "You don't understand, two hundred buttons do me no good. I gotta have two thousand!" It took me three and a half minutes and twenty-seven *Excuse me*'s to get through the reception room to Ray's office.

But no talking to Ray. He was surrounded by reporters from *Newsweek, Life,* the *New York Times,* and even one dapper editor from *Le Monde.* Though they were all maybe four feet from him, he was having to shout his answers over the buzzing throngs, the grinding mimeograph machine, and the continually ringing telephones. Barely visible behind the legs of Ray and the reporters were a half-dozen ten-year-olds sprawled in the corner, silkscreening doves on T-shirts and dabbing at still unfinished banners.

I sat at the phone for most of that evening while the circus around me continued. "Come on," one fellow with camera and floodlights was pleading with someone, "just a little cooperation and we can still make the eleven o'clock news."

By the time midnight rolled around, my jittery nerves were satisfied that nothing disastrous was going to happen. Everything was set. I put the receiver down for the last time and leaned back against the window. The office was nearly barren now. Most of the organizers had gone home for a good night's rest. All the buttons, bumper stickers, posters, banners, armbands, and people who wear them were gone. The coffee canisters used as "contribution buckets" were brimming with bills and change. The floor was a collage of paper and paint, and the only voices heard were the low mutterings of Jeff and cohorts, still sorting out the various schools' block assignments for community canvassing.

I felt the coolness of the windowpane against the back of my head. I was tired, but I felt wonderful. It was closeness I was feeling, closeness for my own life, my own destiny. Somehow the world I lived in now seemed within reach, within touch. Before this night it had been so distant. Except for the enclosed microcosm I call my lifestyle, I felt I had no say in the world. I had no say and no one else really did either. The larger drift of history and human events were governed by those anonymous and invisible forces. Things just happened no matter what I did with the arms and legs and mind that I *could* control. Human beings, the things that laugh and cough and get stomach aches when they're nervous and turn red when they're embarrassed and sometimes feel lonely even on beautiful sunny days, had nothing to do with those forces. All of *those* people had nicknames and funny little fears about who they were and whether or not they were liked. They weren't anonymous or invisible at all. But it seemed that those people had really nothing to do with history. It was only cities and countries and institutions that ever decided anything. "Washington today announced . . ." Brinkley would say, or the Pentagon did this or the Democratic Party did that. Where were the people, I asked.

But this night it seemed clear to me that decisions and events really *were* the makings of people. It wasn't simply the ADMINISTRATION and the ANTIWAR MOVEMENT, two anonymous machines that played give and take in a predesigned game of dialectics. It was people, people that laugh and cough and turn red and feel lonely.

Four months earlier we had been sitting on the floor of a dusty, furnitureless office suite. We were people who were angry about the war, angry that nothing had changed. We were calling other angry people all around the country. "Hey, here's something we can start doing about it," we said and then we called somebody else. And those people called their neighbors and said, "Hey, here's something we can start doing about it," and then they in turn started calling somebody else. Pretty soon millions of people were calling and talking. Students talking to the people across the hall, housewives buttonholing friends at the supermarket, dentists mentioning it to their patients in between whirs of the drill.

On a CBS special the night of the fifteenth Eric Severeid said that the Moratorium had earned its place in the history books. That was nice to hear because it meant history was full of laughs and coughs and red faces and lonely sunny days. It wasn't anonymous and it wasn't invisible any longer. It was genuine living people, lots of them, saying to their neighbors, "Hey, here's something we can start doing about it."

I put my coat on and walked back slowly to Leverett House. The sky was clear and sprayed with stars, and the air was unseasonably balmy. The weatherman had said we would have fair skies through Wednesday. Just once, dear Lord, let the the weatherman be right.

CHAPTER FIVE

"United we stand, but a house divided
is just a crummy duplex."
—ABRAHAM LINKAWITZ,
THIRTY-EIGHT STREET BUTCHER

Shook-a-took-took-took—the rollers rattled along the metal curtain rod as I swept the yellow pleated drapes to the side. It was eight o'clock A.M., an hour I had always considered unseemly for anything other than crickets and nightcrawlers. With the palms of my hands pressed flat against the large picture window, I peered down on Cambridge from my seventh-floor room in Leverett House. The rich blue complexion of the sky, the passersby in their shirtsleeves, the stroboscopic sparkle of the sun off the Charles River all told me that, as I suspected, God too was for immediate withdrawal.

I pushed myself back from the windowpane, sleep still in my eyes and limbs, and fell in nervous giggles back upon my bed. It was the single most important day in twenty-one-and a-half years of living. I could conceivably be forty-three before I would have that feeling again.

From outside the door came the sound of Marcie's prancing feet. She had been up and reading her philosophy and theater books in the other room for an hour. Through the door and with an incautiously full-spread leap she was in the air and a second later on top of me.

"Morning, honey-pie," she had said while landing. Her early morning spunk was crushing me.

"Unchain me, woman. I've people to see and promises to keep."

Indeed, there was no time to lose. The day was already old for the ten thousand Boston-area students who had assembled at six-thirty at various checkpoints around the city to pick up the materials and block assignments for the day-long canvassing. For over an hour they had been going to residential communities, factories, shopping centers, and everyplace else where Americans spend their daylight hours. The leafleting, pamphleting, and door-to-door chatting would continue until the three-thirty rally.

I rose to shower and dress. Jockey shorts, black socks, undershirt, took the undershirt off, Right Guard, put the undershirt back on, wristwatch, dark yellow dress shirt, blue-and-silver striped tie, black suit, clumsy black wing-tips. Hadn't been that dressed up since Freshman Orientation Week when President Pusey shook my hand and told me he looked forward to seeing me again on my Graduation Day. A tender moment, that.

"You won't forget to have the car outside at noon?"

Marcie gave her head a quick, high-frequency shake like and excited kid. One last kiss and I was down the steps.

I crossed the Leverett House courtyard on this unseasonably warm autumn day with a giddy nervousness in my step. An actor who travels to the same theater for several months of rehearsal knows the way perfectly, and yet on opening night it all seems new and strange. And thus it was with me as I headed for our office at 44 Brattle Street. Cambridge was new and strange. All the sights and sounds of the daily city existence carried an added political dimension today. It was a special day and everyone knew it was special. Wherever I looked the evidence was there. Young and old with red, white, and blue armbands that read "Peace Now," students with armfuls of anti-war fact sheets looking for the streets they were to cover, cars with strips of black cloth tied to the antennas, store windows with placards of a dove and the posted early closing hours so the employees might attend the rally. But this was Cambridge, where students and faculty and other assorted antiwar sympathizers abound. In places like this or New York City (where forty thousand of the sixty thousand public school teachers remained home) the support was expected. What was far more significant was the unprecedented level of protest that was occurring *all over* the nation. As one of the organizers of a successful Nebraska rally commented to Bernard Nossiter of the *Washington Post,* "This is Nixon country. If it can be done out here, that's *really* something." It seemed the whole nation was finally stirring from its sleepy acceptance of the nightmare in Vietnam.

When I reached the front door of the office building, I was nearly bowled over by a half-dozen ten-years-olds who were exiting with stacks of mimeographed maps of the march and rally sites. They were taking them out to the streets, where they not so delicately pinned them beneath all the waiting windshield wipers. Just inside the outer door sat a young, pretty volunteer with recently arrived shipments of more paraphernalia—armbands, bumper stickers, posters. Buttons, however, the most oversubscribed commodity, couldn't be had for all the graft in Saigon. Next to the table of materials were neatly stacked columns of rubber ash cans that would be used for money collection along the march routes and at the Common. The girl wore a broad contagious smile, like everyone else that day, that seemed to say, "Hey, we finally got it together, didn't we?"

"Hi, can I give you an armband?"

"Sure can."

She laughed and joked as she helped me fasten the arm-band around the stiff material of my suit. I started up the stairs.

"Have a good day," she called after me. I trotted up the rest of the flight all aglow. It hadn't been since last Christmas season that a stranger had said that to me.

In the main office room a half-dozen of the full-time organizers were relaxing around the television set, sharing a load of Danish rolls and coffee that had just been brought from a deli up the street. One fellow who had been up most of the night mimeographing block assignments for the canvassers was munching on a roast beef and onion sandwich. Working around the clock tends to make breakfast, lunch, and dinner foods quite interchangeable. On the tube was Dave Garroway interviewing Jerry Grossman. Whenever Jerry turned his head to answer, the floodlights glinted off his uncowled baldness, and we could see the bunting of hair that edged his pate like a bib put on backwards.

"Mr. Grossman, you were the one who had the original idea for the Moratorium. How does it feel now that the day has finally come?"

Jerry smiled from sideburn to shining gray sideburn, and said with Boston pride, "I feel like we gave a pahty and the whole country showed up."

Forty-four Brattle Street filled with proud laughter and "Right on, Jer!" "Hubba-hubba, baby!" and other nonviolent war cries, emotional eruptions to take the edge out of caffeined bodies. Wax paper rustled and cracked as more prune Danish and apple popovers were brought out to feed the still hungry, and we all sat atop desks and cabinet files to watch the rest of the interview. Grossman was in fine form. Vietnamization, he said, was a ploy to cover up the administration's intention of lending permanent military support. Jerome Grossman, the successful envelope manufacturer, didn't seem to be quite fitting

my roommates' strict Marxist analysis of the war. When the interview ended we all commented on what was said well and
what wasn't said well, and what each of us would have said that
would have been so much better.

Every so often a phone rang, but mostly it was just small
chatter that filled the room. Except for an unfinished detail
here and there the work was behind us. We all just wanted to
relax and enjoy this especially sunny, mid-October day.

"Oh, boooo! We don't want *him*," someone yelled. Everyone turned his eyes back to the television. Grossman was off and
replacing him in the chair next to Garroway now was Ted Kennedy. Kennedy's office had declined our invitation to speak at
the Amherst rally. Instead the senator chose to appear at one of
those proper World Affairs Club luncheons. But even *that*
crowd was conspicuously quiet when the handsome senator told
them that non-combat troops should be left in Vietnam for
several more years. No one in the office seemed to feel much
kinship for this homestate darling.

"Lot o' bullshit!" someone said and everyone else added
rumbles of "yeah, yeah" the way Western movie extras do when
someone yells, 'Lynch 'em!' My feelings were, as usual, mixed
and still mixing. Intellectually, I recognized all the opportun-
ism and ambiguities of a man who wants to be president. But
emotionally, in those least arguable portions of viscera, I still
held on to the hope that this last of a most attractive family
might live up to the myth that I and millions of others had
constructed for the Kennedys. I resented Edward Kennedy for
not being all the things I wanted at least *someone* in this
world to be, but at the same time I felt a prick of loneliness
when one of the girls rose to shut off the TV with a bitter
"Just the same as all the rest."

The remainder of the morning was passed in reading all
the daily papers that came into the office. Every few minutes
someone laughed and blurted, "Oh, get this," and then shared

some priceless quotation with everyone else in the room. Consensus had it that Agnew was deranged but still a finer man than Joe McCarthy, though not so good as Mussolini.

Around eleven-thirty Grossman arrived back at the office and held a brief press conference. Then we were off to Boston City Hall to join the official reception committee for McGovern. We were fifteen minutes late, but once we were out of the building and in the waiting car Marcie's bold right foot had us skimming along Storrow Drive toward City Hall.

"I don't understand what's with Kennedy," I said to Grossman as we began slowing for the Government Center exit. "I thought he'd take a real lead among antiwar senators this fall."

"Chappaquiddick," he answered simply. He crushed his cigarette in the ashtray and dropped a Life Saver into his mouth. "With Chappaquiddick Kennedy figures he's gotta stay out of the public eye for a while. Believe me, his feelings are with us."

Tremendous good his *feelings* do us! What was to be hurt by speaking out more than he did? He was already senator. What was left except the big white frat house on Pennsylvania? But of course. That's enough for any man to hold his tongue, or at least for some it is. Don't act rashly, wait until you're in a position of greater influence. Now where had I heard that logic before?

When we got to City Hall, we drove around back to the mayor's private entrance. Parked in the driveway was a freshly waxed black limousine. I've been told that with their hectic schedules politicians often get confused as to whether they're being driven to a rally or a funeral. To make sure, they sometimes have to glance at those around them to see which way the lips curve. After okaying it with the guard, we parked the car in a "No Stopping" zone at the edge of the driveway—October 15 immunity. On the sidewalk across the street stood a doctor in full whites with a stethoscope protruding from his

coat pocket. He was handing out postcards that were addressed
to the White House to anyone interested in sending the president a personal message of protest. That day the niftily organized medical community of Boston handed out one hundred
eighty thousand such cards. They were trying to tell Nixon that,
at least medically speaking, bodies aren't meant to be torn
apart.

Jerry, Marcie, and I took the swank elevator that ferried
visitors from the limousine's lower-level garage to the mayor's
penthouse office. There we were to meet up with two others in
the welcoming party and then leave with a police escort for the
airport. It was all so sordidly governmental.

By the time we counted heads on the top floor and got
back down to our cars it was 12:40. That left twenty minutes to
get to the airport. Our car followed snugly behind the chauffeur-
driven limousine, which in turn followed only several yards
behind a squad car that had its red gumball machine flashing.
We sped past everyone, through stoplights, yield signs, anything
that was in our way. Ruthless use of state power. I ate it up.
When we reached the airport we turned off the main artery
to the terminal onto an obscure and narrow road that led us
out to the stretches of concrete where airplanes make their
home. The beige cement reached endlessly in all directions, and
the piercing, high-pitched whine of jet engines was everywhere.
The squad car in front drew a beeline for the gate that received
the American Airlines afternoon flight from Washington, sped
up the last thirty yards, then came to a rubber screeching halt
as squad cars seem to do no matter what the occasion. The
limousine followed. Marcie eased her own car in between the
limousine and one of those Shell tank trucks with the foot-wide
gas nozzles. After turning off the key she whispered to me that
she was repressing an urge to roll down her window and tell
the man with the ear mufflers to "fill it with regular."

We all got out and waited. Within a few minutes McGovern's plane was on the ground and nosing its way toward our cars, but Grossman, the host, was lost making a phone call somewhere inside. I was at the base of the boarding stairs, tousled and windblown, when the screaming engines wound down and the door to the front section swiveled open. First came two young staffers with briefcases at their sides, then McGovern, wearing a sky-blue blazer, earth-gray trousers, and distractingly golden socks, as golden as the endless wheat fields in America's midwestern plains. He looked like someone from South Dakota. No, he looked like South Dakota itself, South Dakota incarnate. "Don't greet him," I told myself. "Harvest him."

"How do you do, Senator."

He took my hand warmly and made me feel right at home, which I guess is what I was supposed to do to him. We walked back to the cars exchanging small talk about the day and the rally. I told him we might have as many as one hundred thousand people on the Common. His eyes bulged and he said, "Gee." A simple man with populist roots—oratory wasn't his forte.

Jerry had finished his phone call and was leaning against Marcie's car, waiting for us. He and McGovern greeted each other as old acquaintances and got into the limousine together. McGovern was assembling his presidential task force, and he wanted Grossman, as one of the leading antiwar organizers, to be on it.

Then, realizing he had forgotten somebody, McGovern got back out of the limousine and came over to the side of our car. As Marcie leaned forward to put the key in the ignition she found a strange hand dangling between her and the steering wheel.

"Well now, who do we have here?" McGovern asked.

Recovering from the initial start Marcie grabbed the hand
that was a quarter inch from her nose and answered, "Oh, I'm
just a driver."

"Uh huh, well isn't that nice?" the senator guffawed, and
got back into the limousine. A simple man with populist roots
—oratory wasn't his forte. Marcie was still shaking her head
and chuckling as she put the car in drive and followed the
mini-motorcade back to the mayor's office.

In another ten minutes we were back in the early afternoon
shadows of City Hall's huge concrete edifice. Hoisted one upon
another, the massive cement blocks, like overlapping dominoes,
fill the air with city government.

When the elevator doors parted at the top floor we were
greeted by the mayor's administrative assistant, Barney Frank,
a throwback to the nineteenth-century Tammany Hall ward-
heelers and city bosses, complete with prodigious belly and
a cigar. He ushered us through the maze of offices to the posh
inner office of Mayor Kevin White.

From expensively wood-paneled wall to expensively wood-
paneled wall lay a juicy thick carpet that made me want to take
my shoes and socks off and squeeze my toes in the under-layers
of fatty mesh. On either side of a glass-topped mahogany table
were two puffy, saffron couches where we all sat down. I sat
forward and crossed my legs to assure that my supporting leg
would be driven all the way to the floor—something only the
world's short people think about. At the end of the table was
a black leather chair that waited for the mayor. The room was
lighted by subdued flourescent rectangles in the ceiling and,
more dramatically, by a picture window that looked out on
nearly all of Boston. From this view one could see a million
people every day walking and riding to work, playing in the
park, stopping at the newsstands, picking and bickering for
fresh fruits and meats at Haymarket. It was a spectacular view

all right, and a delirious feeling of power, probably not unlike the feeling people get just before they jump.

Most of us sat and talked in a library hush while McGovern and a staffer retreated to a corner to go over last-minute changes in his speech. Then Mayor White came in. It was a sweeping, dignified entrance of a gray-templed man that made it clear everyone should stand up. Barney Frank, rolling his cigar from one corner of his mouth to the other, made all the introductions. McGovern and his staffer joined us as we all sat down again around the table. Then rigor mortis set in. Posing smiles were abundant, but the conversation was stiff, like a chipmunk that's been dead for two weeks. Everyone seemed to have a sudden itching attack. While we all sat scratching and smiling, smiling and scratching, Frank popped in and out of the office, bringing the mayor tidbits of information about his city. "You won't believe it out there," he said on one of his trips in as he pointed out the window with his cigar. "I swear the whole goddamn Common is gonna cave in." Those of us with the Moratorium lit up—Mayor White just tugged at his cuffs.

Finally, tiring of the uncomfortable pauses, Grossman reared back and let loose with a spicy one.

"You know, Senator, it really wasn't *our* idea at all to have this Camejo fellow speak today." ("Good God, Jerry," I thought. "Don't bring that up *now*.")

McGovern let the text of his speech drop from his hands to the glass tabletop and turned to his aide sitting next to him on the couch for an explanation of what this was all about. The thirty-year-old staffer, a Harvard Law grad, placed the palms of his hands on his vinyl attaché case and turned the color of a thirty-year-old staffer about to throw up.

"Well . . . you see, Senator . . ." They had both turned toward each other until their knees were practically touching. "Uh . . . we had actually made the commitment to speak in

Boston several weeks before we found out about this other fellow speaking."

"There's *really* no need to worry about this thing at all," I piped up. I was a great one to lecture on the subject! "The guy's gonna give a more radical speech, that's all. No big thing." ("Anyway," I thought, "you'll be on a plane back to Washington by the time he tells the crowd to lynch you.") McGovern returned to jotting notes on a copy of his speech. He had lost that senatorial smile.

Five or ten minutes passed in conversation about the magnificent layout of the new office. Mayor White said it was a beautiful view, and we all agreed it was a beautiful view. I wanted to ask the mayor if he ever got lonely.

When McGovern appeared to have finished repairing his address for the day I launched into what I had considered a rather humorous account of just how difficult it had been to organize the Moratorium in McGovern's home state of South Dakota.

"The entire summer," I said, "I had only one student-body president turn me down flat because he thought the Moratorium was too *radical*."

"University of South Dakota, I suppose?" McGovern asked dryly, clearly in control of his excitement over the story.

"Yep," I answered. "He told me that if the NSA endorsed us then we had to be bad, because the NSA kept sending him letters saying they could help arrange for antiwar speakers to come to his campus, and as far as he was concerned that was the same as instructing him how to organize riots." I cradled my chin between a aspread thumb and forefinger, and pondered an appropriate embellishment over the last time I had told the story with Marcie in the room. "And so finally he just said we had nothing more to talk about and slammed the phone down so vehemently that the receiver bounced off the hook and I could hear him swearing and panting until he hung up a second time." Not a smile from either McGovern or White, and Grossman began coughing. Impregnate a senator's daughter before you rib his home state. I grabbed for Marcie's hand and settled back into the folds of the couch. To hell with where my feet reached.

Not long after that performance it was time to emigrate to an adjoining room where McGovern and White were to hold a joint press conference. No one was expecting the cautious Mayor White to comment on the war, and no one was disappointed. His most controversial statement was, "I'd like to welcome the senator to the Commonwealth."

One of the reporters asked McGovern what he thought of Agnew's challenge to the Moratorium Committee to repudiate Hanoi's letter of endorsement. "If Hanoi were to endorse apple pie," he answered, "are we then obligated to repudiate it?" Halfway through the conference Galbraith walked in and shocked everyone by sitting on the floor off to the side. But by the time the remaining minutes had elapsed, Galbraith had answered three of the questions directed at McGovern and had castigated the Boston press twice, which shocked no one. "I'm sure as you oh-so-omniscient men of the press know . . ." he prefaced one of his answers. Nobody seemed robbed of a fun time when Barney Frank, who had been pacing along the back wall, signaled it was time to head for the Common.

Up one side street after another, the squad cars led us through an oblique route that was intended to avoid any downtown traffic. But few cars were on the streets and the red-brick shops were all but empty. The pulse of the entire city had moved to one great nodule called Boston Common. We reached the park from the rear and parked our cars about a hundred yards behind the stage and scaffolding that had been erected only that morning. The heavy strum of an acoustical guitar and the hoarse rasp of folk singer pulsated from the stage.

A maroon picket snow fence hemmed the semicircular staging area. Inside the fence were pressmen and Moratorium-associated personnel. To wend our way through the crowd from the car to there would have been nearly impossible had it not been for Barney Frank, who grabbed both Marcie and me by the arms and led us with the authority of a locomotive right to the gate. Cops along the way who saw Barney puffing ferociously on his cigar as he tried to drag these two bright-eyed innocents to safety lent helping hands. They liked doing things like that for the City Hall gang.

When we reached the stage, Marcie and I held onto each other and watched from just beneath the scaffolding. Meandering around the stage with note pads and cameras were men from nearly every major newspaper and magazine in the nation. Everyone knew that Boston was going to have the largest Moratorium demonstration in the country, and everyone wanted to be there to cover it. Many of them had been in and out of our Cambridge office as well as the Washington office for the past two weeks. Some of the pressmen had been in so often they felt a kind of personal attachment to what was taking place on this culminating day. One fellow who had been covering the Moratorium for the *Record American*, the conservative tabloid in Boston, had become so engaged to our cause that he came in every night after he had finished his own work hours to help write flyers and press releases, man the mimeograph machine, stuff envelopes, and do anything else he could to aid the Moratorium. "Just don't tell my bosses," he used to say.

Only five minutes until the speeches were to begin, and I still hadn't had a really good view of the crowd. The largest antiwar protest Boston had ever had before this was twenty-five thousand. The men from AP placed this day's crowd at a little over a hundred thousand. I climbed the narrow wooden slats leading to the top of the stage, my heart and toes tingling. At the top step I lifted my eyes from my unsure feet out into the buzzing throngs.

"Oh, Jesus!"

The sight was recklessly spectacular, one of the biggest highs I've every had. From Beacon Street all across the width of the Common people were packing in as close to the stage as they could possibly squeeze. About fifty yards out were three elevated platforms with TV crews, and high above were several helicopters taking aerial pictures. When I looked straight back into the crowd it was like looking at the ocean until my eyes reached the earth's curviture and, rather than saying I couldn't see anything anymore, saying I could see the horizon. The crowd stretched and stretched until it finally disappeared behind the great knoll in the lightly wooded area of the park. The thousands beyond that point couldn't see the stage, and we couldn't see them. But each knew the other was there. That much we could feel.

And we could feel more, too. We could feel the spirit and cause that covered and bound us like a giant net. It was a commonness that started at the stage and extended to the very last person one hundred yards beyond the knoll. It was a spirit that somehow made it not at all strange that sitting on the grass amid all the bearded and sandaled guys and all the bra-less and bell-bottomed girls were businessmen and lawyers in herringbone suits, and women with hairdos. Somehow on this one sunny afternoon none of the colors or lifestyles seemed to clash.

Though they had come in dedicated and serious protest, their spirit was neither morbid nor angry. Their thoughts weren't with the perished lives that could never be reclaimed, but with the lives that could possibly be saved because of this day. The negation of death and destruction was implicit, but the visible, tangible message was the affirmation of life. People clapped their hands and joined in on the songs from the stage, and when no one was singing through the microphones, songs arose spontaneously from the crowd. Toward the front a man who wore on his shoulders a six-foot papier-mâché caricature of Nixon's head danced wildly to all the music.

Several thousand feet above us in the crisp blueness a skywriter was carving a fluffy white peace symbol. Somewhere in the crowd a *Life* photographer aimed his camera toward heaven and snapped. When the skywriter finished his last stroke the crowd exploded into cheers and someone began chanting, "Peace Now!" Within seconds the chant was picked up, at first slowly and then quickening and building to a deafening crescendo, and soon the whole atmosphere was vibrating with one hundred thousand human beings crying, "Peace Now!" We were winning, and I wanted to cry.

The chanting eventually subsided, and the crowd resumed its autumnal murmurings. Somewhere out there one gent was ringing a cowbell. A jet that had just taken off from Logan Airport passed over, and the rumble of burning air escaping from its engines mixed with the contented rumbling of the non-travelers on the ground. Whatever city that plane would land in, the people aboard would still be in the middle of the Moratorium. In New York the masses were gathered at Times Square to listen to speeches by Gene McCarthy and Sam Brown, and on Wall Street thousands of businessmen were holding their own antiwar rally. In Des Moines, Iowa, several thousand housewives were standing on streetcorners handing out black armbands, and in Golden, Colorado, the state's miners and the students from the Colorado School of Mines were readying for a nighttime candlelight parade. In Los Angeles they were listening to Dr. Ralph Abernathy, who had taken up the black man's torch against the war from Martin Luther King, and in New Haven, Connecticut, fifty thousand were assembled on the New Haven Green. From Delaware to Oregon and from Minnesota to Texas the protesters were having their day. All historians agreed that it was the largest national protest in the country's history. No matter where that plane landed, it would still be M-day.

It was three-thirty, and the crowd was restless for the speeches. Professor Everett Mendelsohn of Harvard, the emcee, was about ready to begin. The five speakers were sitting on rickety metal folding chairs at the rear of the platform. Suddenly there was a bustling behind the stage, and within a moment John Kenneth Galbraith was up the wooden stairs and striding toward the microphone. The speakers' committee had bickered for days as to who would be allowed to speak, but as the game of prestige would have it, no one felt particularly inclined to tell the six-foot-eight professor that he wasn't on the docket. One consolation, of course, was that he was probably the only speaker the people behind the knoll could see. It was a short speech, a cameo performance. Hunching over the podium and its mike, the Economist led into his introduction of McGovern with an invocation of the family he assumed would most please the crowd. The name of John Kennedy was received with a subdued smattering of applause, Robert Kennedy elicited larger waves of approving cheers, and the bark of Ted Kennedy's name was met with nearly total silence and even a few boos. On that cheery note the Economist introduced poor ol' George McGovern, who was left with the task of convincing the temporarily turned-off crowd that some senators can be trusted.

To McGovern's credit and smiling relief, he was received with a standing ovation. Students all over the park stood and joined the older people in the warm response. They wanted to believe. We all wanted to believe.

In his first few words McGovern ably put his finger on the spirit of the day. "This is a day both of regret and affirmation," he said. "This is a day not of name-calling or violence or destruction. This is a day that calls not for the politics of revenge but the politics of reconciliation." Then in that first minute of the speech he got to it. "The most urgent responsible act of American citizenship in 1969 is to bring all possible pressure to bear on the Administration to order our troops out of Vietnam *now.*" The crowd responded wildly. In 1968 Eugene McCarthy, the peace candidate, was running on a "negotiations now" platform. This day was the first time they had heard a senator call for immediate withdrawal.

McGovern should have stopped on that note, but he unfortunately had pages more of text to run through. The pity of the speech was the speaker. Poor ol' George was saying all the right things, but was saying them so methodically and so emotionlessly, the trees began to whistle with yawn wind. A simple man with populist roots—oratory wasn't his forte. When he finished twenty minutes later the polite applause started, hesitated, then finally got going again when McGovern reached his seat and there was no doubt the speech was over. The clapping was spasmodic, no heartier than a hundred thousand people trying to kill the same mosquito.

The following Sunday Jerry Grossman was awakened at seven in the morning by a phone call. It was McGovern.

"Jerry," he said. "Tell me honestly. Was I dull on Wednesday?"

Grossman didn't hesitate. "Yep, you sure were."

I felt sorry McGovern didn't have a greater power of speaking to turn on this crowd, and in fact this whole country, more than he did. He hadn't, like so many other politicians, endorsed the Moratorium as a "day of conscience" or a "time of concern," but had endorsed the Moratorium for what the Moratorium meant, a demand for total and immediate withdrawal.

While McGovern quietly climbed down the back stairs of the stage and got into the mayor's limousine, Mendelsohn was at the mike introducing the second speaker, Howard Zinn, a Boston University professor and home-town favorite. Two years earlier Zinn had written one of the seminal anti-Vietnam War books, *Vietnam: The Logic of Withdrawal*. Whatever emotion had been absent in McGovern was certainly all there in Zinn.

His speech was essentially the chronology of America's involvement in Indochina. As a he dealt with each step of U.S. aggression, he leaned his tall, thin body out over the crowd until his chin at the end of the arc was beyond the front of the lectern. He spoke in jagged, stabbing syllables. And as he concluded each step of his argument with a shouting demand for the end of American imperialism, he snapped his body erect like a trackman's fiberglas pole, back out of the reach of his listeners. His dangling black hair lurched from his eyes and forehead, and the crowd cheered him on. Then he would move on to the next parts of the chronology, each time with a leveling of vehemence and volume, but always at a slightly higher plateau than the time before. And each time he would begin building slowly, again curving his torso forward over the crowd, trying to stare every one of them in the eye. And each time he would wrench himself backward at the moment of that argument's conclusion and renewed call for an end to American imperialism. That was always the moment for responsive whistles and cheers from the audience. He was building by layers.

But unfortunately Zinn was soon so caught up in the speech himself that that fine sense of what is enough had been totally buried in his enthusiasm. He quickly passed the allotted fifteen minutes and was soon pushing the half hour. That marker drifted by, and he was then onto forty-five minutes. The audience's stamina had been drained, and when Zinn pushed the hair from his forehead and snapped his spine for the last time the crowd was able to muster only as much energy as Zinn had left them. They had been beaten.

Zinn came down from the platform sweating and exhausted. He rolled his tongue from one corner of his mouth to the other trying to wet his lips. For the past several years he had spent night after night delivering these frenetic speeches against the war. His passion for the subject had never worn thin. Like so many activist professors his life had become increasingly entwined with the war, and every night that he leaned out over the crowd his insides were torn just a little bit more, and he was driven on even harder to the next night's speech. At the bottom of the stairs he smiled palely at his waiting friends and then disappeared with them into the crowd to listen to the three remaining speakers.

The next two speakers were James Breedan, an Episcopal minister from Roxbury, and Kay Hurley, Massachusetts leader in the National Welfare Rights Organization. She planted herself firmly behind the lectern, her feet spread wide, and staggered as though she were ready to run a race. Her style was somewhat to the offensive side of harangue. After the first four sentences Marcie and I decided to head back to Leverett House before the after-rally traffic jam. There we could watch the rest on television.

In minutes we were shooting along the outside lane of Storrow Drive back to Cambridge. The posts of the guardrail ticked past Marcie's open window like a kitchen timer. Past Boston University, past Fenway Park, the expressway bent and wound along the shore of the Charles River. It was five o'clock, and the aging sun left the river's waters a grayish chill. Marcie rolled up her window and the ticking guardrail fell silent behind the glass. I leaned over and pulled a wisp of hair behind her ear, and we both smiled. We weren't just lovers—we were each other's best friend, and that's a whole different smile.

When we got home Marcie parked her car and we walked up to my room to catch the rest of the rally on TV. The Leverett House courtyard, elevators, and hallways were deserted. I didn't think anything could empty the house like that except a Harvard-Yale game. By the time we got the feeble tube on Cheyney's old portable set to light up and the horizontal flicker to obey, Kay Hurley was into the last few minutes of her speech.

She was shouting herself hoarse at the crowd, but was saying little about Vietnam. It was all about welfare rights and the inequities of the present welfare system. Only as an afterthought would she throw in an, "It's just like the injustice in Vietnam." Most felt a general sympathy for her cause, but that wasn't what they had come to protest against this day. A pan of the crowd revealed buzzing impatience. Marcie and I watched it from the bed and buzzed a little ourselves.

Polite but uninspired applause followed Kay back to her chair. Her place at the front of the stage was taken by the last speaker of the day, Peter Camejo, the Venezuelan revolutionary who had had us all ready to write a press release of disassociation. Still a step or two away from the microphone, he started in on his speech. He didn't want a single person to leave the Common before he had a chance to work his spell. The words came in a high pitched, stacatto cadence, and his whole body vibrated to the rhythm.

Vietnam, he said, isn't a mistake but an absolute inevitability of the system.

"And to those politicians who are joining the bandwagon," he continued, "this antiwar movement is not for sale. This movement is not for sale now, not in 1970 and not in 1972." I expected the next shot of the crowd to show five thousand people sitting in front of the platform and ninety-five thousand people heading for the Park Street subway station. But that wasn't so. People were listening and responding. Certainly the majority wasn't agreeing entirely with the revolutionary stance, but they were listening. Camejo bounced and gyrated. His arms flailed above his head, and every so often he ran his hand through his short, curly hair. Had I turned off the sound it would have probably appeared to be a comic mime. But it wasn't comic, because the emotions he was eliciting from all of us were too forceful and genuine. It didn't matter whether we were socialist revolutionaries or not. He made us hate the war perhaps more than we ever thought possible. It was a scourge, a plague—there could be no "timetable" for ending it, it had to be ended now. Camejo spoke with such easy power, it was demagogic and frightening. This was a day of peace, but he made me see just how close the peace in the antiwar movement always is to something far more charged and militant. Our own latent emotionalism and contempt surprises us all. Camejo ended his speech at the peak, and the crowd applauded until their hands were weary.

The people hadn't come to burn down a city, but the "rational discourse" that McGovern had offered wasn't really enough. They were a peaceful group, but a group that wanted to feel their emotions. That, Camejo had given them. The throngs left the Common for home and dinner. Many had plans to attend neighborhood candlelight marches and silent vigils later that night. The closing shot on the television was of several hundred students picking up debris from the grass. As the Boston *Globe* editorial stated the next morning, the Common was left cleaner and fresher than it had been in a decade.

It was five-thirty and growing dark outside. The Charles was now an inscrutible purple. Marcie and I sat at the window silently transfixed. The die-hard pinks and oranges on the clouds' western fringes were losing by attrition. One by one the burning tips were extinguished and one by one the cars migrating from traffic-jammed Boston turned on their headlights. Soon all of Storrow Drive was a crocheted string of car lights, and the river and sky beyond them were black. It was a little after six when we got up and went to dinner.

Everyone had just arrived back from the Common, and the Leverett House dining hall was packed. Marcie and I took our trays of food to a table toward the rear, where we joined a group of friends. Everyone at the table said the day's spirit was so beautiful it was unreal, and acquaintances gave me the "thumbs up" sign as they passed our table. In one meal my head grew ten pounds fatter. On the way out, however, one of my less-than-bosom SDS friends asked with a mock ingenuousness whether we had begun to organize a Youth for McGovern in '72 yet. It was his way of saying he thought we were all using the Moratorium as a political stepping stone. I wanted to suggest he go beat up some dean or throw darts at his father's picture, but thought better of it and passed without answering.

It was a New England autumn night. The temperature had dropped from the afternoon's sixties to a breath-misting chill. Marcie and I went back up to the room to get coats and then walked over to the Cambridge Common. This is a small park near the Harvard Law School where local clergymen had planned a candlelight vigil. Still a block away we could see the tiny, quivering flames moving quietly, eerily about the park, delicate torches shining and then disappearing as the people holding them wove braided paths between the trees. Coming closer we could begin to discern the faces, the dimly lit portraits behind each candle. The faces were solemn and peaceful, faces of people who had found the afternoon's political rally necessary, yet insufficient. These faces were seeking more, seeking some type of spiritual imprint that would make this day, this feeling, more than just one of political protest. They were needing and seeking a religious recourse that would transcend the power of even the greatest power elites. It had been a half-dozen years since I had been in a synagogue, and yet here I was at the vigil, needing and seeking like the rest.

At the edge of the park a priest in his long white and black robes gave us each a thin white candle and lit them for us. Marcie and I took each other's hand and walked silently toward the center cluster of trees where everyone was gathering. Over a thousand people were already there, about half of them students, the other half older community residents. They were all very quiet. When people spoke at all it was only in low whispers.

We assembled in a large circle with four or five clergymen and a bearded folk singer in the middle. Marcie, all aglow from this part of the day that she felt closest to, tugged at my hand and pulled me with her to one of the front rows. The idea of religion in politics excited her. She didn't want to miss any part of it. The first half of the vigil consisted mainly of regular service prayers and hymns, except replacing the organ and choir was the strum of the bearded fellow's acoustical guitar. We all held our flickering candles and read and sang the words from the distributed mimeographed sheets we held in our free hands. Parents holding small babies managed as best they could looking over neighbors' shoulders. No one seemed particularly capable of carrying a tune, but we all sang loudly, and at times the guitarist had difficulty being heard even with the help of the microphone.

When we finished singing one of the younger pastors with long, shaggy hair began talking. It was, I suppose, our little service's counterpart to a Sunday sermon. But he wasn't sermonizing, he was just another fellow like the rest of us, talking about the war. He wasn't trying to give a polished speech from the pulpit. His sentences were rife with ums and pauses to gather his thoughts. No one expected or wanted him to be polished. He was a pastor who happened to live in Cambridge; he was a neighbor of ours, and he was talking to us about the war.

He said he once heard Joan Baez tell an audience that if history had shown nonviolence to be a flop, it had shown everything else to be a bigger flop. He said that he felt perhaps man's history was on the verge of something very new and very exciting. Never before had so many millions of people dedicated themselves so earnestly to peace, especially when in the short run it meant for many a painful stance against their own country. Never before had so many Americans created an atmosphere that affirmed all there was in the world to *live* for. He said he couldn't help feeling that October 15 was a part of an emerging spirit, and that no single day before had he ever had as much reason to be hopeful. We all stood with our flickering candles, listening and sharing. Only from something as momentously tragic as the Vietnam War could there ever have come a spirit so momentously hopeful.

The pastor asked that we all lay our candles on the ground and take the hands of those next to us. Marcie was on one side of me and on the other was a man in his late forties who looked the part of Nixon's "forgotten American." He had a crew cut and wore gray work clothes and a blue zipper jacket. He took my hand and I could feel his rough skin. In that first instant came the awkwardness and conditioned urge to recoil from a stranger's touch, but he squeezed my hand gently and the touch was no longer strange. Our personal lives were as different as could be and yet they were exactly the same.

The man with the guitar began strumming and singing, "All we are saying is give peace a chance." Everyone joined in, singing over and over again the slow refrain, "All we are saying is give peace a chance." The candles on the ground fluttered and dripped waxen eggs in the grass. "All we are saying is give peace a chance." Swaying back and forth like rows of poplars in the autumn wind we sang, "All we are saying is give peace a chance." Over and over, softly, always softly. I stole a glance at the man next to me—his eyes were shining with tears. Perhaps he had lost a brother in the war. Back and forth, "All we are saying is give peace a chance." No words other than that. They drifted out from the park and down the tree-lined streets of Cambridge. "All we are saying . . . All we are saying . . ."

The guitar stopped and the pastor raised his hand out in front of himself. "Peace," he said, and then turned away. We all picked up our candles and walked as we had come, with friends and families, away from the park. Most kept candles burning as they walked through Harvard Square and down the streets toward home. When Marcie and I got to Leverett House we went across the street to the river. We sat on the grass for a while just talking, about the day and about the coming months. She always said that listening to me talk about politics was like taking medicine but with a candy coating. And we talked about ourselves as well. We laughed about how people came up and told us how much our love showed. One girl said we "mooned over each other" so much we were obnoxious. We laughed about her, too. It was getting colder out—we walked snugly together up to my room.

The major networks were having ninety-minute specials on the Moratorium, covering all the day's major activities around the nation. We turned the set on and watched for a while. Someone on CBS was interviewing Hawk in front of the Washington Monument, and on NBC were films of smaller marches in rural towns and a tape of Sam's speech in New York. We lowered the sound a bit and climbed into bed. When they got to the rally in Boston we sank beneath the covers and made love. I wanted to touch and caress the whole world. I wanted to make love to a hundred trillion people and be swallowed in their eyes as I could be in Marcie's. The low hum of the TV was still filling the room when the two of us finally fell off to sleep.

CHAPTER SIX

"I woke up today and found
Frost perched on the town."
—JONI MITCHELL

The night of November 3 Cambridge lay cold and betrayed by a retreating autumn. It had been only three weeks since that warm and peaceful day in mid-October, but three very critical weeks in the seasonal continuum. Those last balmy vestiges of an Indian summer had come and gone, and so had the few days of peak foliage in New England when all the Berkshires in western Massachusetts were a rustling gold and red. Now all the trees were bald and shivering, and on the curbside, strips of grass were piles of brown, leafy crunch and the carcasses of pumpkins left behind by Halloween marauders.

I drilled my hands deep into the torn pockets of my maroon stadium coat and zipped up the front as high as it would go. I left the floppy hood bouncing on my shoulders in stand-by alert. The six-year-old coat was an ugly jalopy of wearing apparel. Marcie said it always made me look as though I were on my way to a high school student council meeting. But this particular night I was on my way to Marty Peretz's home. All of us who had been working in the Cambridge Moratorium office were gathering there to listen to President Nixon's highly publicized and awaited response to the fall antiwar protests.

This night of the speech was clearly the focal point of our anticipations since October 15. The energy level around the office had been very low indeed since that day. We all kept saying, "Well, we just gotta wait to see what the president says." And of course we *did* have to wait—the speech would largely determine the immediate fate of the antiwar movement. But the partial lethargy we were experiencing was also a function of something else, something we didn't care to publicize, even among ourselves. And this was the realization that the expanding Moratorium strategy, the addition of one day each month, simply was not going to work. Nearly every campus coordinator I called had the same response. "Man, I'm practically flunking out of school. I'll be able to go down to D.C. for the Mobe's march, but I just can't hack this every-day organizing any longer." And so it was a continual search for replacements to take over the campus and community organizations. No one seemed particularly upset though by this period of recuperation. The march in Washington, we all hoped, would be enough to carry the antiwar momentum to December. We would then at least have a little time to revise our own Moratorium strategy.

The Peretzes live in the quiet and comfortable section of Cambridge where many of the Harvard professors reside. I got there about a half hour before Nixon's speech. Anne, bulging beneath her dress with yet another little Peretz, draped my zip-up tenement over the already coat-covered banister and ushered me into the warm, painting-filled living room. Jerry Grossman, Ray Dougan, Everett Mendelsohn, and a couple of others were already there, relaxing on the couch and extra chairs that had been brought in from other rooms. I helped myself to the cake and coffee Anne was offering and took a seat near the fireplace next to Professor Mendelsohn.

While more people arrived at the front door the growing numbers inside talked about the possible Moratorium activities for November and future months. Grossman and Mendelsohn and a few of the other people in the room were visibly disappointed by the waning enthusiasm of the students.

"What did they expect?" one elderly woman asked. "That talking to a resident for ten minutes in October would be enough to change his mind about the war? Good grief, people need to be educated, and that takes time!" The gray-haired lady had been in the antiwar movement for decades and she just couldn't understand what young people thought peace politics was all about.

I tried to explain that whether or not students were justified in their impatience, this *was* in fact the situation, and that we would have to think up new activities that might catch the students' imagination. We discussed a few abortive ideas and concluded that the march in Washington would just have to be impresssive enough to take the pressure off the Moratorium to repeat the October performance. And of course in the backs of all of our minds was the hope that Nixon would announce a change of policy that might obviate *all* further protest actions. Then we turned on the TV.

Two soap commercials, then one about the Peace Corps— it stirred memories of the early '60s and the New Frontier— then the president and a slapping realization of what the New Frontier had led to. He sat behind his mahogany desk, smiled, and welcomed us all into his oval. After that the speech was all downhill, at least from our viewpoint.

First, Nixon began by explaining America's original involvement in Vietnam. "We Americans," he said, "are a do-ityourself people—we're an impatient people. Instead of teaching someone else to do a job, we like to do it ourselves. And this has been carried over into our foreign policy." Just a swell bunch we are, bubbling over with Yankee ingenuity and an uncontrollable eagerness to demonstrate modern warfare to those mental paupers in Asia! Everyone sat with narrow eyes, silently cursing the man on the screen who couldn't see us. Marty slouched deep in the couch and with a few choice swear words shoved his thick glasses hard against the bridge of his nose.

After Nixon finished reiterating his election promise to withdraw all combat troops on his own private timetable, though never mentioning the quarter-million non-combat troops that that would still leave in Vietnam, he turned his attention toward the antiwar protests.

"In San Francisco a few weeks ago, I saw demonstrators carrying signs reading 'Lose in Vietnam. Bring the boys home.' " He jabbed the word 'lose' as my grade-school teachers had done in preaching against losing the space race to the Russians. The low blow sent waves of contemptuous shouts across the room. "You motherfucker," Ray breathed quietly into his coffee cup.

Nixon went on, "I would be untrue to my oath of office to be dictated by a minority who hold that point of view and who try to impose it on the nation by mounting demonstrations in the street." Those same grade-school teachers used to point at the brown-and-green 1750 map of the colonies and speak nostalgically of the days of mass assemblies in the town square. I guess we were supposed to have matured from that kind of democracy. Nixon gripped the edges of his desk as though he were about to raise himself to a handstand, and leaned into the camera. "North Vietnam cannot defeat or humiliate the United States. Only Americans can do that." I looked over at Grossman. He was sitting calmly in his suit and tie, slowly shaking his head. Then he looked at the floor and just kept shaking his head. Nixon concluded his speech with the usual plea for unity so the "enemy" would understand the unbending American will.

No sooner had the insignia of the presidency come on the screen than the phone was ringing. It was Sam saying there wasn't much to do other than express our disappointment and continue with plans just as they were. Marty asked us from the den what we all thought. We mumbled our dejected agreement just loudly enough for Brown to hear, and that was the end of the conversation.

When Marty got back to the living room he found us all staring at our knuckles and knees and shoes, not saying anything to anyone. He sat down on the couch next to his wife, Anne, and took her hand. He also apparently, had nothing to say. Finally, Jerry broke the silence.

"All right, I think we've indulged ourselves in enough gloom for one night." No one answered. That only spurred him on to an even brighter tone of voice. "What were we expecting Nixon to say—'OK, OK, you guys were terrific on the fifteenth, I give up, I'm bringing all the troops home and disbanding the army!'?" We let only a few scattered giggles escape, like little kids trying to maintain a good pout no matter how funny or apologetic big brother is being. "We knew Nixon wasn't going to be any pushover," Jerry went on. "That was the whole point of making the Moratorium grow every month. And frankly I think this speech is going to assure that the Moratorium *does* start growing all over again." He looked from face to face—the sulking eyes were beginning to brighten. The idea of Nixon incurring the wrath of the American people for this speech seemed plausible, and now we weren't feeling quite so bad anymore. "The worst thing that could have happened," he continued, "would have been if he had announced a withdrawal of say seventy or eighty thousand men. That probably would have been placating enough to take the punch out of the spirit we've got in this country now."

"That's right," Ray added, clearly won over by Jerry's locker-room pep talk. "That way all the marginal people would have gone over to Nixon's side, but now I think all the people who were hesitating in October are going to be with *us*." That was followed by a fugue of "yeah!" and "you betchya" and "damn right!" Our spirit was back on the sunny side of the manic-depressive curve. It seemed clear to us now that Nixon was shoving the whole country into the antiwar movement. We decided that that would be our statement to the press, that Nixon was being so intransigent he'd absolutely assured us of a snowballing antiwar movement. Ray, a couple of others and I offered to write the press release that night. People began getting up from their chairs.

"One other thing before we go," Helen Rees, our press secretary, said. "The New Mobe people in Boston want to have a joint press conference with us some time this week." That casual statement worked like an invisible drug, bringing everyone to an instant freeze. Nothing like mention of the New Mobe in a room filled with Moratorium people to stir the argument glands.

"I'm so tickled," Grossman said sardonically as he settled back down into his chair. "Why do we have to go in on *anything* with them?" Jerry was against having any official ties with the Mobe, so was Marty, and so was I. Our arguments were chiefly that we shouldn't tie ourselves to a weekend march that could turn into a violent disaster, and secondly that it was important to keep the two organizations separate in the public's mind. We were clearly outnumbered by the other ten or twelve people there who argued for the "unity of the antiwar movement." The ensuing debate lasted two and a half very hot hours.

At one point Marty turned anger-crimson in the face and

jumped to his feet. "You know, there's an old Yiddish saying," he snapped. " *'Er vill tantsen oif aleh chasenes.'* It means you *have* to dance at everyone's wedding, you just can't stand to be left out of anything! Why do we have to join every action taken by every other antiwar group? These are the same guys who walked us into the cop clubs at the Pentagon in '67, and I don't want to have anything to do with them." He pushed up the sleeves of his sweater and plunged himself back down on the couch to the *whoosh* of a compressing cushion. "Ask Sam— these clowns don't even want to let senators or labor leaders speak at the rally."

"Well, I don't blame them," Anne said with almost as much emotion as her husband. She was sitting on the couch next to him, holding their year-and-a-half-old boy in her arms. "It's been too many times that we've worked to build up an antiwar movement and then handed it over to those hypocrites in office." Marty took the baby from his wife and held the little boy high above his head. "I love your mommy," he said, "but boy, is she silly!"

The debate continued with the three of us trying in vain to convince the rest that an intimate tie with the march in Washington could possibly lose us our entire moderate constituency. I heard later through the grapevine that the Washington office was in the same throes of controversy—Marge and Hawk seeking a closer relationship to the Mobe and Sam and Mixner wanting little if anything to do with that group. Of course their decision was far more important, since it was their office that commanded the national attention, but we still felt it important to make the position of our regional office clear to the press. Our watches showed just past midnight, and tempers were beginning to molt their insulating layers of friendship.

Helen Rees began to pick up her purse to go and glared at Jerry and Marty and me. "You don't even know what's at stake, you just make me so furious." She rose from her chair and

cracked her shin against the coffee-table, but refused to acknowl-
edge the pain. "Every day I try to play down the differences
between the two groups and everyday the reporters badger me
with questions trying to find a major split to write about. Just
don't think refusing to have a press conference with the Mobe
isn't going to tell those reporters something."

"All right, all right," Jerry blurted, crossing his hands in
front of his face as a shield. "Don't get excited. We'll *have* the
joint press conference." Helen sneaked a victorious glance at
her backers in the room. "Just so I'm not the Moratorium
spokesman there."

"Don't worry, Jer," Ray offered. "I'll take care of it. Let's
just call this meeting quits before we tear each other's heads
off." We all mustered a reconciling laugh and made our weary
ways for the door. A few of us climbed into Ray's street-creeper
and rode with him over to Brattle Street to begin writing our
press release in answer to Nixon's speech.

We started our think session with paper, pencils, and coffee
across the street from the office at Cardell's all-night ham-
burger joint. By one-thirty we had our chins in our hands and
only one paragraph of half-coherent copy. The busboy, a fifty-
year-old down-and-out fellow, accidentally spilled some cream
on the page while cleaning the table next to us.

"Be careful with that, this is our answer to Nixon," Ray
said with a sleepy, wry smile.

"Oh, a thousand *pardons*," the man answered sarcastically.
"Why don't you just wait a half hour. He comes in here every
morning at about two—you can give it to him personally."

By twenty to six in the morning we had only a drab,
rhetorically predictable statement, but it would just have to do.
Ray left it on the desk for the morning secretary to dictate over
the phone to the *Boston Evening Globe*.

Quarter to six as I trudged down the stairs and into the
early-morning world. I could tell you the sun was weaving

strands of gold and rouge on the eastern horizon, but it wasn't. It wasn't even the slightest bit visible behind that overcast gray mush. It was cold, too, but not enough to splash any wakefulness into me. I was in my Leverett House bed in seven minutes and sound asleep in eight.

When I woke up it was dark outside, but I thought it was still Tuesday. The alarm clock was ringing. Then I remembered I didn't have an alarm clock—it was the phone. I got up and stumbled for the light, then for the ringing.

"H'lo."

"Hi, honey-pie, how ya feeling?"

"Well . . ."—yawn—"let me think." I pulled on a pair of underpants that were lying dead on the floor while I held the receiver pinched between my head and my shoulder. "On a scale of one to ten, about a three-point-two—the high side of shitty."

"Yeah, I saw the speech. Guess all of you must be feeling pretty low."

"Well, some of the people in the office think this is really gonna give the movement an added impetus. But I'm not quite sure how great even *that* is. I mean, like we were really big in October, right? And now we see the government doesn't really have to respond, so what did we really achieve? Success without success."

"Yeah, but if more and more people keep joining, Nixon can't do that much longer," Marcie countered decisively. Then, all sureness evaporated. "Can he, honey?" I didn't know. No one knew. Brown and Meacham were both quoted in the *Times* that morning as saying they were sure that now both of their respective antiwar groups would grow, but of course that's what organizers are expected to say to the press. Like everyone else, they would just have to wait for the reaction of the American people. In the meantime, both Marcie and I had work and decided she shouldn't come into Cambridge until the next day. After hanging up I dressed and made my way to the Fogg Art Museum. The rest of the evening I tried to learn a little something about Impressionism.

The next morning Cheyney left the front section of the *Times* at the side of my bed. As I sat at the edge of my mattress for my usual morning ritual of four and a half minutes of thoughtless, moodless staring at the floor, the paper was right there, framed between my thighs, the first thing my eyes focused on that glorious fall morning. On the front page was an article summing up the nation's reaction to Nixon's speech. The results of the first Gallup phone poll were in—seventy-seven percent of all those who watched the speech now favored Nixon's Vietnam policy. I finished the article perfunctorily as one finishes the last unpleasant minutes of a test he knows he has failed. Then my eyes came back up to the first paragraph, settled, and for the next half hour remained fixed upon the seven, seven, percentage sign. That slow, sick feeling of helplessness and defeat that begins in the stomach was soon wallowing in every part of my body.

It was almost impossible to believe. Not only had Nixon refused to change or even modify the Vietnam policy, but in one televised speech he had virtually turned the country around on the issue. Strong hawks remained strong hawks and strong doves remained strong doves, but that huge percentage of marginal people had been won over to his side. That kind of response had of course seemed inconceivable to us. We were so caught up in the Moratorium and spending so much time among ourselves that it really *did* appear the whole country was with us. We saw Nixon's speech as only another way of saying, "Whether right or wrong, I refuse to be the first U.S. president to lose a war," and it seemed only natural that everyone else would perceive it the same way. But we had forgotten about all the Americans who think, "He knows something we don't know; he's the president and he must know best." A strong, personal plea from the president for support—it's difficult for many to turn down.

Our movement had been so big and so strong, millions of people just like me, getting it together with our neighbors, and the public opinion steadily swinging in our direction as well. Yet now it was totally erased by one half-hour speech by one man. I got up from the bed and began dressing, kicking the newspaper along the way. I pushed each button on my shirt through its hole with a bitter fury as I peered into the mirror above my dresser. I felt disdain and contempt for the powerlessness of the skinny little boy who peered back at me. "Tell me now, little boy, how history moves and turns."

The crowd at Freedom Square surged and retreated like a tidal surf from the sidewalk and curb into the middle of wide Mount Auburn Street, and then back to the sidewalk again. The surges, however, weren't timed by the phases of the moon but by the periodic rumor that the buses were just up the block. No one wanted to be left behind in Cambridge when all the action was in Washington. But soon people grew weary of hoisting their knapsacks and sleeping-bags on their shoulders to get in line only to learn that it was just another city bus fuming its way down the street. They would sit on their bundles along the curb and wait until they saw the big silver Greyhounds with their own eyes.

The low-fifties weather made it warm enough for me to keep my thinly-lined beige jacket unzipped. I assumed the weather in D.C. would be at least as warm—there was certainly no need to take that cumbersome, maroon thing. All I held was a bag lunch of B-L-T's and warm milk that I had picked up in the Leverett House dining hall that evening. It was now quarter of twelve—the buses that had been chartered by the New Mobe, the Peace and Freedom Party, and SDS were scheduled to load and leave by midnight.

Marcie was already in Washington, staying with her roommate who lived in Bethesda. She had gone only because her roommate had pleaded that they hitch down together. Marcie had been promising since freshman year to visit her and her parents at their home, and this seemed as good a time as any despite Marcie's parents' advice to steer clear of the potentially violent weekend.

"Oh my God, don't tell me Ken Hurwitz is actually going to take an SDS bus down to Washington." The voice, like a rabbit punch, came from behind. It was Mike, an unhappy little revolutionary that had been in my encounter group course the year before. Everytime I saw him he delighted in baiting me for my affiliation with the Moratorium Committee. In fact, my roommate, Cheyney, was about the only SDS'er I could talk to without feeling I was a warmonger. "Don't you even know," Mike said with a grin, "that SDS chartered buses only so we could talk to people on the way down, and tell them what phonies the New Mobe and the Moratorium are?"

"Yeah, yeah, I know all about it." I actually thought it pretty clever of SDS to charter buses so they'd have a chance to talk to students, but I wasn't about to admit that to *him*. I looked up the street, hoping one of those buses was on its way now.

"Aren't you afraid if you listen to us," he asked with a persisting sarcasm, "you might lose some of that allegiance to Sam Brown and the Democratic Party?"

"You're absolutely right," I conceded. "Eight hours on a bus with you could turn me into a John Bircher." I turned away, pondering the events that led me to go to Washington in the first place, thinking perhaps I had made a wrong decision.

At a press conference shortly before November 15, Brown

announced that the four national Moratorium coordinators were going to join the New Mobe march on Washington as individuals. By that time it was evident that there was little interest in further Moratorium-type actions. Their individual commitment, however, soon became organization policy as Brown and cohorts decided it would be better to have *some* say in the march than to have no say at all, and therefore agreed to help the organizationally and financially troubled New Mobe on a *group* basis. Because they were lending desperately needed assistance, from rally logistics to organizing of the marshals, the Moratorium leaders eventually gained some leverage within the Mobilization. One example was the decision of the New Mobe's steering committee, meeting in their headquarters one floor above the Moratorium's office, to exclude politicians and labor leaders from the speakers' list. Within minutes of hearing that, Brown was upstairs on the ninth floor and, with the help of Meacham and several other Mobe moderates, made sure that decision was reversed. And thus as time went by the Moratorium leadership became more and more involved in helping plan and control the weekend march.

So, as nearly all of the month's focus came to rest on Washington, and as I heard more and more the argument that the best way to prevent massive violence at the march was for all the nonviolent activists to be there, I finally decided to join the pilgrimage. By then, however, it was Thursday, November 13, and most of my friends had already driven down in cars to join the single-file March against Death in front of the White House.

"Not all is lost," Cheyney announced that night as he stepped out of the shower and raised his forefinger high in the air. "Seventeen and a half big ones, and you get to ride down with us. Give you a chance to hear the *real* issues."

"Yeah, yeah, just give me a ticket," I said. "And tell your friends I'm not an agent."

An so it came to pass that I was waiting at five to twelve on a Friday night for an SDS bus to Washington. A couple of minutes passed, and then came the buses, about fifteen of them, one right behind the other like an assembly line of big, shiny boxes. Everyone picked up his weekend gear, while Cheyney and a couple of others moved in and out of the crowd with bull-horns, instructing which ticketholders to take which buses. I climbed into one of the buses halfway back in the parade and settled into a soft reclining seat next to a window. I put my bag lunch on the floor in front of my seat. For the next ten minutes people played musical buses, switching and then switching again until everyone was in his proper place. The bus driver looked at his watch and pulled the lever next to the wheel. The door hissed shut. He seemed indifferent to the purpose of this night's trip; it was just his job to get us to Washington by eight-thirty the next morning.

The caravan began rolling, and we were on our way. No sooner had we reached the entrance to the Massachusetts Turnpike than the bus was divided into sections for "discussion groups," each group being led by one of the members of SDS that was aboard. Our group leader squatted in the aisle and began talking to the eight or ten of us about how he thought the General Electric strike and the War in Vietnam were one and the same.

"The world is made up of bosses and oppressed workers," he said. "You have to side with one or the other." Memories of Kenyatta in El Paso flashed in my mind. Our group was divided with a couple more disagreeing than agreeing with the SDS position. Voices on both sides grew steadily more truculent as the conversation continued. The boy next to me, however, remained mild and beyond provocation.

"I may just be a naive freshman," he said, "but I really think the world is a bit more complicated than that. I mean I really believe there are a lot of forces and factors that determine people's opinions other than their positions in industry. Like why is the bulk of antiwar movements always made up of upper-middle class people?" Marxist analysis seemed to fall down on that one, and the only answer the group leader could muster was a semantics game of redefining the "antiwar movement." At first I joined in on the argument, but after about two hours I grew bored and tired. My roommates and I had talked about nothing else all year. I turned my head toward the window and closed my eyes.

"Don't you see," I heard our group leader instructing in the background. "Goodell was appointed by Rockefeller and Rockefeller is one of the capitalist pigs that's responsible for the war, so any antiwar bill introduced by Goodell just *has* to be a fake." The voices grew more and more distant as I bundled my mind in privacy and sleep. I began singing "Urge for Going" to myself but the words were soon too heavy. I was fast asleep by the third verse. I awoke once briefly at about four o'clock to the shuffling of people leaving the bus to get cokes and hot dogs at a coffee shop somewhere in New Jersey. But we were soon in gear again and I was once again dozing off, still on the third verse. "You see the geese in chevron flight/Flappin' and a-racin' on before the snow./They got the urge for goin'./They got the wings to go." The high-pitched drone of rubber spinning over pavement swirled into my ears and out into the open fields of Delaware.

When I awoke again it was ten past eight and we were on the outskirts of Washington. The sun ricocheted a nearly blinding glint off the silver metal of the bus in front of us. Most of the people in our bus were still asleep, their heads and bodies drooping to one side like unstrung marionettes. I picked up the sack lunch between my feet and eased myself out past my sleeping neighbor to ask the driver to drop me off in front of the HEW building. We had to go right past it on the way to the area around the Capitol where all out-of-town buses were to park. I had told Marcie over the phone the night before that I would meet her at 10:00 in front of that new building. When we got to the closest corner I hung onto the rail from the lowest step and waited for the bus to come to a stop. The doors hissed open and I hopped out onto the curb.

I couldn't have been worse at anticipating the Washington weather. The sun was shining brightly, that's true, but the air was a frigid thirty degrees and the wind whined like a siren through the naked trees on the Capitol mall, hoisting leaves and debris as it went. I zipped up my light jacket, but it didn't help much. The wind still burrowed its way inside on top, and down below turned my blue jeans into frozen cardboard. I crossed the street to the grassy area where other early arrivers were making ready for the day. Some were dragging camping equipment out of cars, others were busy hammering cold, rusty stakes into unreceptive ground and yanking on the ropes of little green pup tents. Still others were unloading boxes of radical and underground newspapers and leaflets. Whenever someone offered me a flyer I stuffed it between my elbow and the side of my body, and quickly returned my hands to their warm pockets. Soon I had a half-dozen pieces of paper clamped to my side and pressed flat by the wind against the front of my jacket.

After a couple of minutes of walking, my stomach began to clamor for a morsel or two. Turning my face away from the wind I peered into the brown paper bag that was tucked inside my other arm. During the hours it lay at my feet on the bus I must have dreamt I was José Greco—The B.L.T's were now two undecipherable balls of mayonnaise, welded bacon and bread mush, and tomato paste, all shot through with fragments of cookie shrapnel. I dropped the bag into a big, yellow trash barrel. Then I walked back to the HEW building.

One of the doors in back was open. I spent the next hour keeping warm and talking to a few of the guards. One of them told me that as long as the protests stayed nonviolent he was all for them. Another one, though, a young black man, said that every time we antiwar people left Washington after one of our protests the riled up cops would take it out on the blacks who lived in the city.

"You know we can't just pack up and leave like you kids," he said. "You can bet there aren't going to be many brothers out there today, 'cause it just means twice as much hell for them the next month." This was something that Stuart Meacham had mentioned once on our trip in September, that civil rights leaders from this predominantly black city often objected to the antiwar rallies planned in Washington because of the police backlash that would be inflicted on the ghettoes for a month afterwards. Meacham had confessed that he simply didn't know the solution, but that as long as the government was in Washington that that city just had to be the target of antiwar protests. But the guard was right—as in October, not many blacks could be seen this day.

Around quarter of ten I ventured back outside to the front of the building. A National Guard transport passed, and two of the guys hanging out the back of the truck flashed the V. I didn't want to take my hands out of my pockets, and so did the best I could with my elbows. I think it wound up being an M. After about five minutes of calisthenics and letting my nose drip on the front steps of HEW, Marcie and her roommate, Andi, showed up with Kleenex and food. I helped myself to both.

The three of us walked to the large plain of grass at the base of Third Street, where the march was to begin. We were all three of us arm in arm against the piercing wind. Tens of thousands were already there, and thousands more were gathering every minute. The bright colors of the heavy woolen jackets, the sound of rubbing mittens, the reddened cheeks and windwatery eyes were all reiminiscent of a late-season football game.

People gladly pressed against one another for warmth, and no one person could see everyone else. New Mobe button and poster salesmen mingled through the crowd selling their wares. Nearly a quarter million dollars were collected that day.

At eleven o'clock the blue-armbanded marshals began moving people into phalanxes, always appearing apologetic for their positions of authority. No one there was big on orders. Then came a hush and I could hear the familiar voice of Senator McCarthy coming over the loudspeaker, as usual in the low key, matter-of-fact tone of Jimmy Stuart. I don't remember everything he said, but it was a good strong speech that punctuated the mood of early-morning unitedness. When he finished we applauded for a full minute and then another half just to keep warm. Then we were off, section by section, row by row, falling into place behind thousands and in front of thousands more. We all locked arms and covered the street from curb to curb until we got to Pennsylvania, where marshals stood on the center line, smiling and wishing us a good day and trying to keep us on just the one side of the wide avenue. After about forty minutes of marching, our painfully kempt rows began melting, and soon we were just a rolling mass of protoplasm, trying to keep up as best we could with the rest of the cell.

All the way down Pennsylvania Avenue we marched in the shadows of the gray government buildings that made the day fifteen degrees colder. Whenever we reached a corner we were on sunlit pavement, but within another twelve steps we were again in the shadows. Cops and guards popped their heads out every so often from atop the buildings and a few executives could be seen peering out the windows of the Justice Department. Whenever one of them was spotted everyone started chanting, "Peace Now," and holding up his hand in the V. I joined in, but there was a certain inhibition and reluctance in my voice. This always happens to me when I am in crowds. I can marvel at and be made to feel good by the sound of a crowd, but it's always from a certain distance. Never does my voice assume the bellow of the all-consumed. Perhaps because of a certain cynicism or a certain clutching at my individual being, I am always in part the third-person journalist. It can sometimes be an uncomfortable feeling of not fully belonging, but, just the same, it can never be helped. I squeezed Marcie's hand. It was already half past one.

We were nearing the corner of Pennsylvania and Fifteenth, where the march route was per government orders turned away from getting any closer to the White House, where the thirty-seventh president of the United States was watching NCAA football on the tube. The route was instead directed up Fifteenth Street on toward the Washington Monument. The feelings in my fingers and toes had all long since gone on sabbatical.

It was quarter of two when our feet finally touched the frosted grass of the mall. There in front of us was the Washington Monument, the ivory white obelisk that I fantasized was driven up through the ground from Asia until it pierced the America sky. Spread out along the ground for hundreds of yards in every direction were the two hundred fifty to three hundred thousand people that had come from all over the country for this one afternoon's rally. We managed to find a spot where we could just see the stage and were barely within earshot of the speakers. There we huddled, trying to remain below the wind's line of fire. The long program of speakers and singers had begun over an hour ago when the lead marchers were arriving. At the moment Arlo Guthrie was on stage, his curly brown hair to his shoulders, singing his antidraft "Alice's Restaurant." The last time I had seen him perform was at the memorial concert for his father in Carnegie Hall. There he had sung Woody's "This Land is Your Land." I don't know if any of us believed it was our land anymore.

After Arlo came Curtis Stocker, a Vietnam veteran who was active in G.I. organizing. No one was able to move the crowd like this relatively unknown activist. "Over there, Mr. President," he said pointing across the river to the Arlington Cemetery, his voice beginning to quaver, "there is your silent majority." He turned in the direction of the White House. "Just a piece of advice." His voice was rising. "Bring our boys home now, Mr. Pres-i-dent"—he spit the title—"or pretty soon they'll be coming home all . . . by . . . themselves." The crowd began its standing ovation before he ever got to the last word. The thought of such disobedience on a massive scale was one of the most appealing types of revolution this crowd could conceive of. The applause followed him all the way off the platform.

The long list of speakers and singers continued. I sat stolidly for an hour and a quarter, my spine cracking at every change of position like brittle bamboo. At three o'clock I declared the cold officially unbearable and suggested we leave. The opposition from the girls was predictably minuscule. On my first attempt up I found my jeans solidly attached to the iced-over blades of grass. My second attempt, however, was totally successful, and soon the three of us were clomping down Fifteenth Street, looking for a drugstore to warm up in. Around H Street we found a Rexall and there spent twenty minutes at the dirty-book rack thawing and chattering alternatives to how to spend the rest of the day. I wanted to visit my old friends in the Moratorium office and so decided to meet the girls back at Andi's home in Bethesda later that night. They caught a Maryland bus just outside the store and I ran toward 1029 Vermont just as fast as the stalactites hanging from my hips would carry me.

When I reached the building I found the outer glass doors locked with a two-by-four through the inner handles. I cupped my hands around my eyes like racehorse blinders to cut the reflecting glare from the street and peered in at the several dozen people standing around the elevators. A circle of mist expanded and contracted on the smooth, glass surface to the rhythm of my breathing. With two crisp raps of my knuckle one of the fellows standing at the nearest elevator looked up and began walking my way. He was a six-foot-five mountain in blue jeans and a dirty V-neck T-shirt. His face had the texture of asphalt. I stepped back from the doors and the circle of mist was sucked into a dot like the light from a television set that's just been turned off. He removed the wooden bolt and swung the door open.

"Thanks a lot," I said, desperate for the beast's friendship. He didn't answer. "Mighty cold out, mighty cold." I nodded my appreciation again and started past him. Without moving any other part of his body he lowered his hand and caught the width of my chest between his thumb and baby finger.

"Whar's the fahr, lil' frind?"

"Beg pardon?" I asked with the trace of air he had left inside me.

"Ah was arskin' whar ya thought ya was haidin'." He had a nice firm, friendly grip around my ribs as though he were going to squeeze the answers out of me the way he squeezes toothpaste out of a tube every morning.

"Oh me, I was just going up to the Moratorium office." I tried to smile, but it was one of those faint, scared-shitless expressions.

"Ya gotch yerself a parss?" He swept his tongue across his upper gums and showed his teeth, irregularly spaced and angled like the kernels on a rotten ear of corn.

"Well . . . uh . . . no, but I never needed one before."

"This ain't bafore, lil' feller. We spectin' some trouble from them wharther people, an' it's mah job see we don't." He probably didn't know that much about the Weathermen, but boy, did he look ready to beat the crap out of them! "Ya jes gimme yer name an' wait down hare whal I call up." I did as the mountain asked and waited next to the wall-directory of office suites just outside the elevators while he called upstairs on a direct phone.

The scene in the lobby was a bit like a Hollywood premiere —reporters with cameras and notepads and flocks of young hangers-on, all being told by other guards that only so many people could go upstairs at a time. Every now and then young men with trenchcoats and walkie-talkies moved hurriedly in and out of the elevators. They were part of the marshalling system that Sam had set up in conjunction with the city police and federal government. All three parties kept in touch with one another and kept track of trouble areas through the walkie-talkies.

While the head guard was chatting with several curiosity-seekers and taking his time about calling upstairs, a younger, official-looking fellow with a pass pinned on his lapel stepped out of the crowd and into one of the waiting elevators. I recognized him to be the Chicago-area coordinator whom I had met once in September.

"Robbie," I called with a sudden burst of feeling for this near stranger. "How's it goin'?" I walked into the elevator and grasped his hand. His face told me he was desperately close to recognizing me.

"Hey, where you going?" I heard one of the guards call at me. I continued shaking Robbie's hand while my other hand pressed the 'Close' button. With no seconds to spare the metal doors slid shut and we were on our way. I wanted to get up in time to intercept the mountain's call and tell him to throw that Hurwitz bastard out of the place. While the elevator ascended I reminded my companion of our brief meeting and thanked him for his dumbfounded assistance. On the eighth floor we both stepped out.

The transformation of the Moratorium office was now complete. A five-room office suite had been sprouting and reproducing until it now covered the entire eighth floor; a staff of six

was now sixty. People ducking in and out of the hallway, carrying messages and answering phones; the faces around me were
all strange. Not knowing where else to begin looking for my
old friends I started with the rooms that we had occupied during the summer. I peeked discreetly into each room but found no
traces. The rooms were all being used now as storage depots for
the mounds of buttons and bumper stickers and fact sheets and
all the other materials the Moratorium had ordered at its peak
in October in anticipation of coming winter months of morato-
ria. A secretary coming in to use the Xerox told me that most
of the people I was looking for like Marge and Dick and Hawk
were still at the rally but that Sam was somewhere in the
building. I thanked her and made my way into the maze of
new offices at the other end of the hallway.

Strangers were milling about in the reception room. One
fellow in a blue denim jacket and jeans was haranguing the
group about the growing amount of revolutionary fervor in the
country. He insisted that within a year everyone in the movement would be underground.

"You can see it already," he said. "Turn this country upside
down and you know what you'd find?"

"Canada?" I offered meekly. He snarled in disgust and
went on with his prediction—something about millions of
revolutionaries falling out of the woodwork in every city. I went
to the other end of the room and sat down. I picked up the
day's *Post* to pass time, but it wasn't long before I heard a familiar voice coming through the closed door of the room a few
yards in front of me. It was the soft and perpetually hoarse
voice I had grown to respect over the summer and had heard
innumerable times on the radio and television since then. I
pushed the door open.

There in a swivel chair was Sam, phone in one hand, tunafish salad sandwich in the other. Seeing me in the doorway, he
raised his hand to wave and—*thud*—a lump of tunafish salad

was on the floor. When he got off the phone he turned to me with a big smile.

"How's it goin', Ken? Have a seat." His tone was, as always, of sincere cordiality, but with markedly less energy than usual. I pulled up a chair next to his desk.

"Well, my personal life is just fine—it's the Moratorium I'm little worried about." Sam nodded, but that never signaled agreement, only that he would like to hear the rest. In between his next dozen phone calls I told him that most of the people in the New England area felt the Moratorium Committee should exit graciously, that the masses weren't about to participate month after month and that it was probably time for new directions. Many of the organizers with whom I had talked indicated that as long as mass participation was quickly dropping to zero, they would like to begin working at a very low-key, low-publicity level on the '70 elections. Sam juggled the sandwich from hand to hand, alternately licking the legacy of mayonnaise from each and continued nodding right up until the end. I closed on the word *election* and he stopped nodding.

"First of all," he said "I think it's still too early to talk about the elections. But secondly, I think we're going to see a revitalization in these coming months. Nixon's speech was just a temporary setback." He had to reach deep into his reservoir of spirited salesmanship as he outlined all the ways he thought Moratorium activities could be tied to Christmas in December. I shook my head at every suggestion. Sam was so caught up with the job of having to be the optimistic leader he was beginning to think and sound like a press release. Everyone is a newspaper reporter and must be made to believe that everything is just dandy. I sat for the most part silently, and at the end could muster only a "Well, maybe." I found it nearly impossible to say to Brown or even to admit to myself that our movement was beginning its slow, downward death spiral. I wanted to be persuaded that what we were doing was still useful to the antiwar cause and worth the time and effort. At least for now, I was willing to accept that indeed there was *some* outside possibility of winning over Nixon's silent majority with our present tactics and strategy. But inside I could feel the gnawing of dishonesty and self-delusion.

Sam seemed weary, perhaps from too many discussions about the Moratorium's future. Several months earlier he could have flopped in peaceful obscurity, but now the pressure of national prominence made every decision a potentially apocalyptic blunder. His eyes were cradled in dark circles, and he seemed fidgety from lack of sleep. Sam Brown was dangerously close to being swallowed by the role of Sam Brown, successful activist who must do and say everything he thinks people expect him to do and say. He rubbed his neck for an apparent stiffness and turned on the pocket transistor radio on his desk to listen to the rest of the rally. Pete Seeger had just finished singing, and now Dave Hawk was at bat. He was nearly hoarse with shouting, giving a fairly hard-line speech about "U.S. imperialism all over the world." The little tin grating over the radio speaker vibrated with every garbled *s* and *p*. Brown squeezed the pen he was holding harder with each of Hawk's radical slogans and shook his head at the floor.

"Oh Jesus, Hawk," he muttered. "How can you be that dumb?" Turning to me, "He *knows* he's the Moratorium representative out there. How can he give a speech like that?"

"You two didn't go over the speech together?" I asked.

Brown shook his head no and flicked off the radio angrily. "I think we're going to have a lot to talk about when he gets back." The patchwork coalition was coming apart at the seams.

For the next five minutes Brown's time was taken up with reports over the walkie-talkie from marshals at various checkpoints around the city. Federal and city officials on the same communication system were also listening to those reports. Everything so far seemed to be calm. Then came a knock on

Sam's office door followed by the appearance of my mountain-guard friend from downstairs. He passed over my presence with a shrug and turned to Brown.

"You seen anybody 'spicious hare?" he asked.

Brown shook his head.

"Wahl, thar 'bout twenty cops downstairs say a bomb thraet's jes been made hare."

My stomach turned into a tiny lead anchor. I instinctively jerked my eyes toward Sam's desk and my mind's eye saw a flash and a thousand gray metal scraps on fire being hurled into our eyes and faces. I just sat there, immobile, staring at the desk while fantasies of violent death plunged their way through my brain. An office full of flames and screams turning to helpless whimpers. The whole idea of someone *actually* planning and effecting my death was so totally incomprehensible a sensation. For one moment that sensation genuinely possessed me, one instant of nausea and horror that somehow, perhaps perversely, verged on euphoric fascination.

Sam threw his pen on the desk, more angry than frightened, and followed the guard out into the reception room. He then passed calmly from room to room, telling everyone who did not have absolutely vital business to please leave. Of course, *everyone*, vital business or not, should have vacated, but that same irrational disbelief affected him just like the rest of us. About four or five of us remained in all. We went from office to office, a madness in our method, sliding open drawers and peeking in file-card shoe boxes. Someone would find a strange metal box and get panicked, but then discover that it was just full of old newspaper clippings or phone messages. We searched for maybe half an hour all the while Brown related to us his hunch about who might have made the threat.

Apparently, the day before, several of the Weathermen's national leaders had come into the office, demanding to talk to Brown. They sat down with him and a couple of other Moratorium organizers, and after some minutes of discussing their political *Weltanschauung*—namely, that the revolution should start with killing one's parents—they demanded of the Moratorium Committee what they called "a sign of fraternal solidarity." More specifically, they wanted twenty thousand dollars or else they would make trouble. Brown has always been pragmatic and willing to listen to and deal with all ends of the political spectrum, but just the same he has always drawn the line at psychopaths. He nodded all the way through their conversation and terminated it with a simple, "No, thank you."

We were lucky. No bomb had been planted that day, perhaps because the Weathermen hadn't really wanted to plant one, but more probably because they hadn't had the chance. Soon everyone was allowed back into the office and was going about normal routines. But the Weathermen and friends hadn't quite finished their adventures in mock revolution. The long rally had finally ended, and it was near dark outside. Reports were now coming over the walkie-talkie of roving bands moving up and down Constitution Avenue, smashing windows and taunting the police. The police were responding with rounds of tear gas and the stronger pepper gas. As is often the case the reaction was at times indiscriminate. Cops were reportedly boxing large groups, including hundreds of passersby, into intersections where they would then shower them with the gases; at the same time several hundred police were sweeping across the rally site, ripping out phones, mikes, and amplifiers beneath the stage and arresting many of the rally logistics people present, including Bill Hanley, the Woodstock sound expert who had set up the sound system for the rally.

Many of the organizers returning to the office were caught in the crossfire. They came in, their eyes tearing and their faces puffed and red. Their clothes carried a trail of acrid fumes, and soon all of us in the office were rubbing our eyes. The messages on the walkie-talkies between Brown, the Mobe leaders upstairs, the marshals on the street, and the cops continued. At one point several hundred of the rampaging demonstrators gathered at Fourteenth and I, only a couple blocks from our office. The frantic voice of the marshal at the scene crackled and screeched through the little gray walkie-talkie on Brown's desk.

"They're in an awfully ugly mood, Sam . . ."—crackle—static—"They've just been gassed and they're still throw . . ." —more static—" . . . ocks and bottles . . . hold on Sam . . . lock up the buildi . . . they're heading for Vermont, Sam . . . they're heading for the office!"

I ran to the other side of the office and opened the window looking out onto Vermont Avenue. Within thirty seconds of that report sirens filled the air and at least two dozen squad cars and motorcycle cops came from all directions to a screeching halt in front of our building. I could hear the shouts and clamor of the crowd just up the block, getting louder and closer. The voices were filled with hatred, uncontrollable, venemous contempt for the liberals and left-liberals they felt were more counterrevolutionary than the nation's conservatives who they believed would actually hasten the upheaval. Most of these radicals came from liberal families and liberal colleges, and now we were the surrogate target for their perpetual indignation and hatred. We were now their strawmen, their phonies "hiding behind rational dissent," and like anyone we judge more harshly because they're closer to us, we were the demons in their romanticized world of political purity. The voices raged to the sound of breaking glass.

But they never came any closer. Several cordons of police were formed up the block and eventually the crowd was dispersed. I leaned my head out over the window ledge into the cold black air, looking down at the cops below and listening to the fading voices of the crowd. The idea of police being needed to keep one antiwar group from tearing apart another antiwar group sickened me.

"Hey, get your head out of that window," I heard someone behind me shout. "Or have you forgotten Chicago?" I heeded the warning and pulled the glass panes shut. Everyone in the office was still a little tense, but trying to get back to normal business. Voices remained low for some time, but eventually the atmosphere turned to one of relaxation, if not sheer relief. The "Fall Offensive" was over. Marge had gone straight home from the rally, but Dick was back, and we talked for some time about our respective girlfriends. He had been my "good listener" all last summer and was now quite happy to hear how solid things were between Marcie and me. Hawk was back also but was really too exhausted to talk for very long. He just sat in a corner chair with eyes closed and his head tilted back. I had never seen him so thoroughly drained. Mixner stopped in, gave me a thin political smile, and disappeared.

In the meantime, Brown was on the phone with Richard Blumenthal, his liaison in the White House, who was arranging for extra buses to get everyone out of the city as quickly as possible. The White House would pick up the bill.

When most of the sirens fell silent and the city was restored to quiet I got a lift to Bethesda where Andi and Marcie were nervously waiting. I said goodby to all my friends in the office and warned I'd be back before long. The Washington streets were eerily deserted, and I breathed easier when we got into Maryland. It was nice being back around trees and grass that no one thought of picking up to assault you with. By the time I got to Andi's home I was dead tired. My political tales of adventure would have to wait until morning.

But when our alarm clock buzzed at eight the next day I didn't feel much like talking about the rally or the Weathermen or anything else vaguely connected to politics. And it's some

kind of queer day when I pass up the opportunity to embellish
one of my stories for a captive audience. But I just wanted
to get in the car and enjoy a sunny day's drive back to Boston.
And that's exactly what we did. Andi was in the front with her
boyfriend, and Marcie and I stretched out in each other's arms
in back. We lay on our backs, looking at the inverted tree
branches and telephone poles and wisps of clouds as they passed
through the curved rear window, talking about nothing except
us. We joked with just a touch of seriousness about what our
kids would look like and laughingly debated about whether
we would get delicatessen food on Saturday or Sunday mornings. It was our updated way of playing house. We talked about
marriage without *really* talking about it. But we enjoyed doing
it, and squeezed each other tightly and said "I love you" with
our eyes the whole trip back. It was a wonderful, beautiful day,
that sunny day in November. The long drive back passed
quickly, and much too soon it was dark outside and we were
turning off the highway at the Cambridge exit.

CHAPTER SEVEN

Come on people now.
Smile on your brother.
Everybody get together,
Try to love one another right now.
—HIT SONG NOBODY SEEMS TO REMEMBER

Anyone who has lived in the cold north knows the slow, erosive destruction of winter. It is the time when the earth's most powerful elements shift and transform, and put all of the previous spring and summer's constructs to their severest, most telling test. The winter months harbor no spite or vengeance, but only a matter-of-fact, unprejudicial duty to sort out the ephemeral from the permanent, the labored stragglers from the chosen. December, January, and February—they are the months of ruthless selection.

I could see the pattern best when I was home on a Christmas vacation visit to our cottage on Cedar Lake. The patterns of destruction were everywhere. The concrete steps we had built at the base of the pier were broken and crumbled by the ice, and were hanging pitifully from the shore like dead flesh. And those steel waterpipes that we had drained and thought so secure were found out by the melting and refreezing ice crystals and were cracked and splintered like a plastic pen beneath a car wheel. One piece was totally shorn and lay half buried in the snow and frozen ground. An icicle fang hung from its broken end.

And that seemed to be very much the pattern of destruction. It was the demise of only the rock and steel and concrete and heavy, inflexible branches. The little saplings around the lake bore no such fate. They accepted the weight of the snow and bent with it like an archer's bow, and there, with their tips nearly curved to the ground, bided their time until spring. Those clever bastards *knew* how to play the game. They knew the Rule of Bend.

But many of us didn't, and, like the steps and pipes and walls, we were sorted out by the winter and marked for a slow, insidious collapse. That gradual winter erosion that *I* faced came on all fronts. Perhaps the most devastating to me was the piecemeal disintegration of my relationship with Marcie. It began in early December, but it wasn't for some time that I even realized what was happening, or at least admitted to myself that I knew. Like all emotional upheavals between two people it started with the nearly inconspicuous, nearly forgiveable little spats. In November we had spent a great deal of time with each other, and Marcie had even begun mentioning with a modicum of seriousness the prospect of marriage, a subject I had already brought up several times before. But that was the final and unbearable closeness that released the repelling chemicals. Neither of us could sustain the level of commitment. Marcie recoiled and the long trip down began.

But I refused to believe we weren't "right for each other." I insisted we were going through a stage that all couples experience and that eventually it would pass. Marcie suggested we date other people while we continued seeing each other to relieve some of the tension, but I refused. I remained adamant that that would be admitting our relationship was wrong, and that we would then never resolve our problems. I was the unmoving concrete, the inflexible branch; I saw rigidity as strength and refused to alter our relationship even temporarily. And so we stayed together and of course made up after every argument, but never with total resolution. The resolve was only in part, the other part going toward another added layer of corrosive resentment. Over the winter the layers were added, one piled atop the other, and eventually the weight was too much.

It was the middle of February when Marcie decided to break off the relationship. But of course matters are never quite that simple. Three weeks and one day later she again showed up at my door. She said she was lonely and miserable, and wanted to give it another go, and I certainly wasn't about to throw away another chance. When she came that day I threw her coat and purse and ugly, floppy rainhat on the bed, and draped my arms around her neck. I just wanted to look at her. I no longer had that euphoric feeling of solidity, that we were two half souls just wandering around this earth, absolutely meant for each other, but what else could I do? She was so much a part of my life, my habits, my daily existence. It was now the fourth of March, and Cambridge was beginning to thaw in the warm breezes. We were hopeful. What else could we be?

It was about that same time that the national Moratorium Committee decided to try to resurrect the antiwar spirit of the fall. The Moratorium had also been a winter casualty. During those months the coordinators in Washington had tried desperately to adhere to the original strategy and keep Moratorium activities alive month after month. Rigid and unswerving from the original plan. But the attempt was futile. Even by late November and early December the masses of participants had begun to peel off like the concentric layers of an onion, and soon only the small, unnoticed core remained. In Washington the staff was back from sixty in October to about eight. In our Massachusetts office only a few people came in a couple of times a week to work. In other cities small groups of organizers stayed on to coordinate a blood drive here or a fast for peace there. By the end of February even these token gestures had dwindled, and the Moratorium was an all-but-forgotten movement.

It seemed that Nixon knew the game of politics far better than we did. After his hard-line speech of November 3 his actions became slightly more conciliatory as he began to speed up the withdrawal of combat troops. Never was that pace of withdrawal fast enough to alter the general nature of the war, nor was there ever a promise to remove the quarter million noncombat troops, but just the same his actions were always *just* enough to appease the great majority. He was a paradigm of the flexible politician, the man who could remain on the same general course, committed to propping up the Thieu-Ky regime, but always deviating and modifying at exactly the proper moments and to the exact degree to remain just ahead of his opposition. Richard Nixon knew the Rule of Bend. That's why he lived where he did on Pennsylvania Avenue.

But we in the Moratorium were still trying to convince each other that perhaps, just perhaps, we could salvage our movement that had been begun nearly a year ago.

"We're going to make it April 15, tax day," Sam announced with the usual optimism on a late February lunch visit to Leverett House. "I think the economic impact of the war is really being felt now. The country is ready to move again." The other student organizers around the table and I exchanged unconvinced glances. Our nods were silent and laced with skepticism. Sure, we'd give it another whirl. What else could we do?

And so beginning in March we again started the long haul of organizing for another day of protest. Consensus was that it should again feature an afternoon rally on the Boston Common. I had heard the April 15 date bandied about as early as January and had, proving my ability to learn from history, reserved the Common in my name for that day. Knowing we had the park permit, the Student Mobe in Boston was more eager than ever to join forces with us and help organize the rally. Together we cranked up the machines and began the month of phoning, leafleting, and postering.

But the spirit in the city was markedly different this time around. Now about only half of the campus coordinators with whom I spoke showed any kind of enthusiasm. The other half responded with, "Do you honestly think peaceful marches and rallies do any good?" I was asking myself the same question, but of course as an organizer I couldn't afford to admit to such doubts. "We can't just escalate the militancy of our tactics every time we get put down," I answered. "We have to have some kind of basic faith in what we're doing." I, too, was clinging tenaciously to the original concept and strategy. And they answered, "All right, this *one* last time."

Over those next six weeks of organizing it became clear to me that the great coalition of last autumn had fallen apart. Many of the students had grown more militant, and this was reflected in the speakers list that was chosen. Each antiwar group in the city that was helping plan for the day was allotted one choice. Whereas Camejo, the Socialist Workers' Party speaker, had been the most radical choice last October, the SWP representative this time was far outlefted by people such as Doug Miranda, a New England official of the Black Panthers, and John Froines of the Chicago Conspiracy. Froines was chosen by NAC (November Action Coalition), a local group that was in the same political bag as SDS and was rumored to be planning on using Froines to lead an after-rally march to Harvard Square for a night of "trashing" (i.e., window breaking, arson, looting). But they denied this, and as long as they were attending the organizational meetings, we couldn't very well deny them a choice of speaker.

Our own project of keeping the more moderate community residents in the movement was failing miserably. All of our dove politician friends refused invitations to speak, from Kennedy on down to every "peace candidate" in the state running for Congress. They all sensed the growing militancy among the young and no longer cared to associate themselves with the present condition of the antiwar movement. Many of us in the office felt betrayed—betrayed by the men who talk of keeping the movement nonviolent and constructive but who, just the same, refuse to take the lead when the situation gets tight. Four days before the rally we still had no main speaker who could draw the older, community people. Again with a dilemma, I gave Marty Peretz a call at his office.

"Marty . . . uh . . . I was . . . uh . . . wondering if maybe, well I thought that maybe you could . . . uh . . ."

"Get McCarthy to speak on Wednesday?" he finished the sentence for me.

"Yeah, well, some of us here thought it might be nice if he could come." My enthusiasm was no more charged than if I had been deciding on a new color for our toilet paper.

"Oh?" Marty said with a friendly kind of sarcasm. "I was under the impression no one there much liked McCarthy anymore." A week earlier Ray Dougan had told him that as long as McCarthy kept speaking in terms of America's helping form a coalition government in Saigon rather than totally withdrawing, he wouldn't have much sympathy of most of the area activists. "What happened to all your other heroes like McGovern?" Marty was sparring with me. He knew very well that ever since McGovern had gone out to Wyoming a month earlier to campaign for Gale McGee, one of the Senate's most virulent hawks, *against* a peace candidate, he had fallen out of favor with most of the New England Moratorium people.

"All right all right, I get the point," I said. "The fact is, they're all the same. Last fall the politicians stepped all over each other to get on the bandwagon, and now what?! As soon as their constituents become passive, *they* become passive, too."

"Now, Ken, you're acting childish." Marty was amused by my ranting.

"That's right, that's exactly right, I'm childish. But someday when I'm a big people"—Marty couldn't help laughing—"I'm serious, Marty, when I *am* I really hope to feel the same way and expect our elected friends to just *once* stick their necks out."

"Like students, I suppose?"

"All right, I agree. Students are in an easy position to be self-righteous. We have nothing to lose. But that doesn't answer the question." A long pause—I could almost see Marty stroking his beard.

"What's this I hear about SDS rushing the stage? I really don't care to rope Gene into a rally like that." It was true. We had denied SDS the right to have a speaker at the rally, and now they were publicizing plans to rush the stage. The growing hostility between them and us began at a late winter New England antiwar conference that the Student Mobe had sponsored. There SDS pushed through a resolution (that my roommate, Cheyney, had co-authored) to bar Moratorium-type liberals from speaking at a spring rally. The Student Mobe, however, knowing that we were going ahead with our own rally on the Common, dropped out of their own conference and joined forces with us. SDS had tried to cut off the moderate faction and had failed. And when they realized they had failed they demanded to have one of *their* speakers at our rally. But we were no longer in the mood. They had tried to eliminate us from our own rally, and now we felt no obligation to include *them*. Free speech, we all agreed, means letting them speak at one of their *own* rallies, not at one *we* worked to organize.

"Don't worry, Marty, if McCarthy shows, I *absolutely*
assure you that no one will rush the stage." I made the promise
so calmly that for a moment even *I* almost believed I could
deliver on it.

"All right, I'll call him tonight and get back to you tomorrow." He sighed deeply and hung up.

For the next two hours of that afternoon and another
two that night I talked over the phone with Cheyney, who had
taken an apartment in Boston since his suspension from Harvard. I tried negotiating some type of compromise that would
keep the rally as peaceful as possible. Cheyney was personally
against taking the stage by force, not so much on moral grounds,
but mainly for the tactical reason that SDS would come off
looking very bad in front of thousands of antiwar protesters.
But he said he was outnumbered by the other leaders in SDS
who were determined to have a speaker on the stage one way
or another. The SDS argument was essentially that even though
it was *our* rally that *we* were organizing, they had the only correct
analysis of the war and of our society and therefore they had
the right to be heard and we did not. It was the backbone of
SDS's logic for everything. The conversation between two old
roommates was jagged with tension and mistrust. We were
political enemies, and that fact was strangling our personal
friendship.

But our attempted compromising was all for naught anyway. Ray Dougan and Bob Bresnahan, the Boston leader of the
Student Mobe, were very much against yielding to SDS's form
of blackmail.

"Look," Ray lectured me that night, "if they had asked
rather than threatened I might feel differently. There are
going to be other speakers up there just as radical as SDS, so
they can't claim political oppression. I just don't buy their
arguments. I used to be in SDS when it was first founded,

but that was before their politics consisted wholly of second-grade temper tantrums. So I'm just for telling them no."

And Bresnahan was even more averse to the idea. He saw his own Student Mobilization Committee as a viable contender for replacing SDS as the leading student organization on the left and was already making plans for SMC marshals to "defend the stage." My argument for paying the small price of appeasement in order to obtain McCarthy was totally destroyed the next day when Peretz called back with the message that McCarthy "just wasn't interested." The final answer to SDS, then, was no.

The last days before the rally passed in mounting tension, confusion and for me, nearly total absurdity. I sat on the phone, making calls, trying to help piece things together, but all the time knowing it was a useless, irreparable mess. Literally no one was signing up to do community canvassing, no major anti-war politicians would be speaking, SDS was laying plans to take the stage by force, and the November Action Coalition was allegedly organizing for the burning of Harvard Square. And on top of this it was clear that the great numbers involved in October all over the country simply weren't going to duplicate their efforts on this fifteenth of April. This time around, the Moratorium was going to be smaller, lacking cohesion, and perhaps even violent. Just the same, I went through the motions. I held on just the way I held onto every argument-filled day with Marcie, even though I saw my own actions as desperately absurd. I was like a doomed man clutching at the armrests of his seat while the airplane falls from the sky. "Hang on tight," I told myself.

Not that I particularly cared, but April 15 was a sun-filled day in Boston. We all knew that the weather's only significance was that it would determine the exact degree to which this day would fall short of October 15. No matter what, the evidence would show that over the last six months our movement had not expanded or even maintained its position, but had contracted —fatally. In Washington, Brown and friends were already preparing for a press conference to announce the disbanding of the Vietnam Moratorium Committee. Excepting a sudden change in events, the day would determine only how graciously the Moratorium would take its leave.

It was a little before two o'clock when I left for the Harvard Square MTA station to take the subway to the Common. I saw the time on my roommate's clock—it had been a month since I had had the conviction to wind my *own* watch. Marcie was back in my room at Leverett House, trying to finish a paper for one of her philosophy courses. When I left she looked up from the desk to kiss me on the cheek, and said that she would probably come down to the rally a little later. For the past several weeks our relationship had consisted mainly of her pursuing her interests and my pursuing mine, all punctuated with friendly yet estranged hello and goodby kisses. No longer did I talk to her about my feelings of political frustration and questioning, and no longer did she ask. We were becoming two strangers, tied only by our shared memories and habits and fear of letting go. Without looking at her, I said that maybe I'd see her down there, and then walked slowly down the flights of stairs to the street.

When I reached the Common I found about twenty thousand people already there, sitting on the grass in front of the stage, listening to the pre-rally singers. The air still held a touch of early spring nip, and most of those gathered wore light sweaters and jackets. They were predominantly young, more so than in October. The doctors and lawyers, housewives and career women who had come out six months earlier were hard to find this day. And within the young students that did come the change of mood and condition was evident. Few were smiling. Most looked as though they were doing exactly what they had said over the phone they would be doing—giving it "one last go." Few of the faces exuded that brightness of belief that had covered the city last October. The great majority there were still pledged to nonviolence, but their growing frustration was beginning to eat away at the faith behind the pledge.

Added to this majority of frustrated and directionless moderates was a growing covey of confirmed radicals, the ones who were more than eager to present the revolutionary alternative to the disenchanted. They stood around in groups, frightening bitterness in their faces, holding NLF flags and anti-Moratorium posters. The members of SDS were handing out leaflets stating that after the third speech the stage would be taken over so Fran Weindling, the SDS representative, could speak. I read the flyer and tucked it in my pocket. The next leaflet thrust at me was by courtesy of the November Action Coalition. It urged everyone to march back to Cambridge after the rally for a more militant protest. The motto was "Stay in the Streets." The graphic design at the top was an arm thrust high in the air, with the hand gripping a rifle. I folded the paper neatly and filed it in my other jacket pocket.

I wandered back behind the maroon-picket snow fence to the stage area. Ray Dougan and John Gage, the rally logistics man, were busy studying the eleven-man speakers' list while Bresnahan strode about like an army general lining up his 240-pound SMC marshals just inside the snow fence. He was giving them last-minute instructions on how to look mean and ugly, and if that didn't dissuade SDS from charging, how to lock arms and fall back in a tight ring around the stage. The agreement among ourselves was that if that tactic *still* didn't hold off the charge and their speaker *did* get on stage, she would be allowed to speak rather than be removed bodily.

I joined Ray and John in their own little strategy huddle. John had the speakers' list in one hand, the SDS leaflet in the other.

"O.K., it says they're going for the stage after the third speech. So it's simple, we put two of the black speakers in the third and fourth positions. That's *got* to spoil their plans."

Ray laughed nervously, embarrassed yet intrigued by the sheer cynicism and vulgarity of the idea that we all shared. But he nodded his agreement, knowing as well as John that for SDS the black man was the second most golden calf, just behind the "worker." They wouldn't dare wrest the microphone away from someone in either one of those categories.

It was 3:00, time to begin chipping away at the long list of speakers. The crowd had been growing steadily and was now about 65,000, a respectable size, certainly, yet a predictable forty percent below the one in October. First to take the microphone was Florence Luscomb, an eighty-three-year-old women's lib representative. She was a dear old lady who some decades earlier had been a member of the suffragettes' Jeannette Rankin Brigade. Women's lib wasn't anything new to her. Her aging voice quivered and the loose skin around her wrists jiggled, but she shouted her demands and slapped the lectern with the best and youngest of them. A gutsy old lady, and the crowd loved her. I spotted Jerry Grossman, who was standing at a rear corner below the stage, and joined him to listen to the rest of Florence's speech.

When she finished the crowd applauded, but then before the second speaker could begin, the chant of "Free Bobby Seale" rose up from the pockets of radicals scattered about the Common. They were already restless, and Grossman was visibly unhappy. Walking across the park before the rally, he had passed one group of students after another that were arguing over whether they would "stay in the streets" after the speeches. He looked more somber this day than I had seen him in a long time. He recognized as well as the rest of us what was happening. Many of the older people had dropped out from the cause, and the younger students were more split than ever over the issue of violence. Jerry looked out at the crowd and frowned. He could feel the tension that was ripping apart his original idea for a massive, peaceful coalition against the war.

"You think many of these students may come back around and help with the elections?" he asked me. I ran my hand along a bar of the stage's metal scaffolding and averted my eyes from Grossman's, and looked out at the enigmatic faces beyond the snow fence.

"I don't know, Jerry." I snapped my forefinger against the metal with a *ping*. "It's hard to tell you what they're thinking when I can't even tell you what it is *I'm* thinking." I shifted my eyes back to Grossman. He looked troubled and disappointed. The impassioned voice of the second speaker, the Socialist Workers' Party candidate for governor, was vibrating in the gray metal amplifiers behind us.

Then, while the speech continued, there came a commotion of voices as about twenty people bustled through the gate behind the stage. In the middle of the group was Abbie Hoffman in a green satin shirt with his wife and two kids. He was surrounded by an entourage of young, blond political "groupies" and a couple of photographers. Gage looked down from the stage with a grin and came over to the corner just above Hoffman's head.

"Say, we really didn't know you were coming today," Gage said. Hoffman seemed a bit embarrassed by his own uninvited appearance.

"Yeah, well I was just in the neighborhood . . . and, uh, . . . well, you know I just live down the road" (meaning Worcester, an hour and a quarter drive on the Turnpike from Boston) "and uh . . . I just thought I'd wander up the road a bit and see what was happening." He hoisted his little girl atop his shoulders, and looked up at Gage. The sun behind the platform made Hoffman squint.

"That's O.K., Abbie," John said. "Things are cool." He looked back down at the SDS leaflet in his hand. "How about if you speak fourth? That's two from now."

"Oh, that'd be just super, man. I'll wait right here."

John left and the rest just stood around while Hoffman play-boxed with his kids. "Come on, photographer man, take one of my kids beating the crap out of me." He swooped up his kids with both his arms and kissed them each on the tops of their heads, and the photographer turned away. Then, spotting Grossman, he put his kids back down on the ground and came over to where we were standing.

"Hey, Jer," he said, "How's my man?" I did a quadruple-take. These were the last two activists I thought would be friends. But to my total amazement, they had known each other for some time. In 1962, Grossman was campaign manager for Professor H. Stuart Hughes of Harvard, who was running as a "ban the bomb" candidate for the senate against Ted Kennedy. The Worcester coordinator for the campaign was Abbie—a little straighter then—Hoffman.

"Hi, Abbie," the fifty-five-year-old Grossman said with a sheepish smile. "How's it going?" Hoffman had in the meantime lifted himself up on the scaffolding, and was swinging freely like a kid on jungle bars.

"Oh, just real super, Jer. How's your team been doin'?" Grossman stood with his hands in his business-suit pockets and grinned.

"Abbie, I'm one of the few who remembers when you were young and conservative." Hoffman had now draped his legs over a bar and was hanging upside down from his knees.

"Yeah, Jer, now I'm just old and responsible." Both he and Grossman burst into laughter. "Well, man, I guess it's

time I start writing my speech." He curled from the waist
and reached for the bar above. Then he pulled himself all the
way up onto the stage and sat there on the corner with his legs
crossed. Several thousand people close to the stage now saw
who was here and let out wild cheers. The word soon passed
and then everyone in the park was cheering. The speaker at
the lectern waited a half minute, then continued. All the while
the SWP speaker went on Hoffman sat on the corner of the
stage waving and mugging at friends and admirers.

In the meantime a couple of hundred SDS'ers had moved
to the fore of the crowd, and their front-line squad leaders
were pressed with their shoulders and chests snugly against the
bending snow fence. Many wore white helmets and heavy boots.
Just on the other side of the fence stood fifty good sized SMC
marshals, not a smile among them.

But what I had thought would be a chilling scene of confrontation now struck me, like many of SDS's acts, as a melo-
drama of mock revolution. There they were, all decked out
in their Sunday riot gear, determined to "liberate" the stage
just so this unknown Fran Weindling could give a five-minute
speech that would be received by a rally crowd's usual wandering inattention. They all looked like Captain Comet. Their
faces were fierce, and their determination was boring through
the tinted visors of their helmets. Serious business, this insur-
rection. "Remember Peking, remember Havana, remember the
Boston Common! Huzzah!"

The second speaker finished, and SDS began with their
rally cry—"Let Fran Speak, Let Fran Speak!" In the middle
of them was Fran. I couldn't tell from her lips whether she
was saying, "Let Fran Speak," or whether she was modifying it
beneath the din to "Let *me* Speak," Over and over they
chanted, their shoulders heaving to the rhythm, their faces
turning red. Fifty years from now Fran will tell her grandchil-
dren of her story—known by sixty-five thousand people as plain

old Fran of "Let Fran Speak" fame. She will tell new acquaintances, "You remember me—Fran?" And when they don't respond she will become more vehement and begin ranting, "Fran! I'm Fran . . ." and finally she will blurt out, "of 'Let Fran Speak!' " And then they will become flushed with contrition and say, "Of course," and apologize, and she will feel much better.

Just as the troops began surging against the cracking snow fence, Gage, with a smile on his lips, ushered the National Welfare Rights speaker to the podium. She was a black woman of about forty. The SDS chant stopped in an instant, and the troops edged back from the fence. It was like holding a cross up in front of a platoon of vampires. They remained in a quiet sulk for the duration of the speech. But when she finished, the roar began again. "Let Fran Speak . . . Let Fran Speak!" The mass of bodies pressed against the fence, and the marshals on the other side locked arms. Then came one gigantic rush of revolutionary flesh and the fence lay splintered beneath the "feet of the people." The outnumbered marshals fell helplessly back to just in front of the stage, fending off the SDS'ers' wild punches, which were for the most part missing their targets and landing with crunches and yelps on the metal scaffolding. None of the upper-middle-class kids beneath those helmets knew much how to fight.

On the stage meanwhile Gage had handed the mike to Hoffman who brought it with him to the front of the platform like a Las Vegas entertainer.

"Yeah, yeah, yeah," he snarled. "Fuckin' PL"—i.e., Progressive Labor—"always with the same crap. Let me tell you something, you PL dupes. Anyone who throws a bottle or takes a swing at a rally to end the Vietnam War is a pig!" Cheers bellowed from the great majority of the crowd. Hoffman continued with his lecture to SDS while they continued throwing missed punches just below the stage. In the meantime Fran

Weindling had worked her way to the side of the platform.
She looked up at one of the stagehands who was sitting calmly
on a folding chair, totally stoned and completely oblivious
to what was happening around him.

"Hey, can you give me a hand?" she asked. He looked
down into her innocent blue eyes and said, "Sure." But just
as he began pulling his fair damsel up, Bob Bresnahan spotted
the inadvertent treason and raced beneath the stage's metal
supports to where Fran's legs were now dangling three feet
above the ground. He grabbed hold of her lower half and began
pulling. And so there poor Fran was, a crumpled speech in
her hand, her dress torn, and two fellows on the same political
side stretching her body over the edge of the stage. Finally,
with one surge of energy the stagehand, pulled her out of
Bresnahan's grasp and into a heap on top of himself on the stage.
Fran got up, threw back her long blond hair, and strode over to
Hoffman. Gage went over to Abbie from the other side, tapped
him on the shoulder, and asked him to give Fran the microphone.

Hoffman shrugged his shoulders and handed the mike over
to John, who in turn held it and its long rubbery cord out for
Fran to take. The Moratorium Committee was baring its van-
quished jugular. Like sixty-five thousand other people, Hoffman
was totally confused as to who was on whose side. He scratched
his head and walked to the back of the stage.

And then came Fran's speech, not half as exciting as what
it took to give it. She started out by saying, "You've been
listening to a lot of crap, but now I'm going to tell you something different." And that was the last "different" statement she
made. Except for a castigation of the "united front" theory,
her class analysis of the war was virtually identical to that of
the SWP speaker, and in fact, of the speaker before him as well.
Nothing new or fresh or vaguely inspiring. This isn't to say it
was a *bad* speech, but only that it was like ninety-five percent

of *all* rally speeches—neither good nor bad, just something
to do once you have a lot of people together. It seemed both
sides should have been embarrassed at all the fuss that was
made. When she finished a third of the crowd applauded, a
third booed and the other third woke up. Fran walked off the
stage with an oh-so serious expression as if to say, "All right,
we can head back up into the hills."

She was barely down the steps at the rear of the stage when
Hoffman was again out front, picking up on the performance he
had begun five minutes earlier. He grabbed the hand mike from
its stand and began pacing from one end of the stage to
the other, tugging at the red twine he used for a belt.

"Boston, the home of revolution and independence," he
said in his nasal mock lament. "Boston, Boston, Boston—and
look at the way you're living." He pointed to the John Hancock
Building behind him, the large concrete rectangle with a tall,
tapering broadcast tower perched on top. "Will you *look* at
what you're living with?" he pleaded. "That tower is a fuckin'
hypodermic needle." Waves of laughter. "John Hancock was a
revolutionary!" Hoffman screamed. "He wasn't any fuckin'
insurance salesman." More thunderous laughter and applause.
Abbie Hoffman, the politico, Abbie Hoffman, the entertainer,
each disguised by the other, the man who had become the
national symbol of cultural more than political revolution, had
the crowd in the palm of his hand.

"Don't you remember Paul Revere?" he asked. "There was
Paul standing on the banks of the Charles when he looked up
at the church and saw the big strobe light. He got on his motorcycle and rode out to Concord yelling, 'The pigs are coming!
The pigs are coming!'" Hoffman leaned out over the front of
the stage. "Right on, Paul Revere!"

And so the show went, Hoffman pacing, mugging, squat-
ting, pacing again, swearing, jumping, and all the time exhort-
ing people to begin freeing themselves before they talked about

freedom for others. And he talked about revolution, but the one
of culture, not of guns. Many times Cheyney and I had discussed people like Abbie Hoffman and had agreed he was an
anathema to both of us, a clown who was taking people away
from "genuine politics." But now, at least that afternoon, I
felt differently. Hoffman's speech, admittedly a grandstand
performance, was the closest the afternoon came to capturing
the best of the cultural spirit in the antiwar movement. Of
course the Abbie Hoffmans of the world have their own brand
of hypocrisy and inconsistency like the rest of us. They haven't
become all love and music beneath their skins yet either. But
that's irrelevant. It's their visions we can't afford to be without.
He didn't talk that afternoon about what split us but about
what we had in common. It was the closest April 15 came to a
spiritual as well as physical coming together.

But the harmony was short-lived. The revived spirit was
no more than a glint, an aside for old times' sake. The rest
of the afternoon was the long, inevitable tumble. Each succes-
sive speaker was more miltant than the next, and the divisions
in the crowd became more and more apparent. The radicals,
grown in strength since the fall, were anxious for the end to
the afternoon so they could have their riot and confrontation,
while many of the moderates began leaving early, disgusted by
the tenor of the day. One of the last speakers was Doug Miranda of the Black Panthers.

"You can't just hope and sing for peace," he shouted.
"You've got to fight for it. And that means you white students
better be ready to pick up guns and help us off the pigs!" The
radicals cheered and the moderates recoiled and shouted "no."
But Miranda was in no mood to soft-pedal his message to win
the majority. He was content to see the line drawn right there
to find out who was the "problem" and who the "solution."
His voice was defiant and filled with contempt. The revolution
is at hand, he said; we have to choose our side, he said; we have

to fight and kill for peace, he said. Fight and kill for peace—
Nixon logic inverted for consumption by the left. Finally several
hundred students toward the front stood up and began chanting, "Peace now, Peace now." Radicals nearby tried to shout
them down, unsuccessfully. "Peace now," they continued.
Several thousand more stood up and joined them. They were
trying desperately to guard and protect their fragile yet still sur-
viving belief in nonviolence. Miranda paid them no heed
and kept right on.

"It's gonna be a class war or a race war," he shouted
through the mike. "You decide."

"Peace now," they chanted.

Somewhere in the air between them the students' idealism
and Miranda's vows slid past each other. They had lived in
two different worlds and their perceptions of what was required
to change that world were commensurately disparate. The moderates chanted, the radicals shouted, and Miranda raised his
fist and proclaimed, "Power to the People," then walked off
the stage. There were neither boos nor applause, just noise.
Everyone was shouting at everyone else.

In the midst of this chaos the last speaker, John Froines of
the Chicago Conspiracy Trial, took the microphone. He spoke
for only about twenty seconds, just long enough to urge everyone to join NAC's march back into Cambridge. "Stay in the
streets," he said. "*Everyone*, stay in the streets." Then he jumped
off the front of the stage to join the demonstrators. I stood and
watched with Grossman and John and Ray and several others
while the thousands cleared the Common. The great majority
headed for the Park Street subway station to go home, but several thousand massed at the corner of the park for the long
march through the streets to Cambridge.

We gathered up the wires, amplifiers, and speakers, and
rolled up what was left of the trampled snow fence. A couple of
blocks away we could hear the shouts of "Free Bobby Seale."

A sound truck near the front was instructing, "Walk quietly—wait till Harvard Square. We're going all the way." The NAC leaflet had said the march would culminate with a demonstration outside the Cambridge City Hall, which is about a mile and a half before the expensive business district of Harvard Square. But now it was clear the NAC leaders were planning on taking the march "all the way."

Soon the shouts grew faint and finally disappeared as the two or three thousand people moved down Beacon Street away from the Common. A row of motorcycle cops were in front, a busload of police slowly following. Those of us who stayed to clean up the Common were all very quiet, absorbed by our own confused thoughts and emotions, wondering exactly what it was that we had done this day. Every now and then John broke the silence by quietly asking someone to take care of some after-rally detail. Within a half hour everything was cleared, the sky had grown dark, and the only sounds were those of the 6:00 traffic in downtown Boston.

I walked alone to the Park Street subway station and got on the train for Cambridge. Most of the people on the subway car with me were much older. It was the tail end of the rush hour. The man sitting across from me was buried in his trench coat and newspaper. When I sat down he lowered the top corner of the paper and glared for some moments at my jacket. I had forgotten the button I was wearing, a large amber plastoid with a red fist grasping an olive branch. The slogan on it was, "A Not So Silent Spring." The man shook his head and returned with a satisfaction to the latest pronouncements of Spiro Agnew. The button I was wearing was, like my feelings, ambivalent. The red fist *and* the olive branch—which did I feel closer to? I didn't know. I felt only disdain for the radicals who rushed the stage, but what about the ones heading for Harvard Square? Didn't I share much of their frustration? I did. Of course, I did.

But except for that shared frustration, I didn't really feel close to much of anything. For a year we had been organizing people around peaceful, inoffensive tactics. It was the road I had believed in and followed. Now it seemed apparent I had missed the dead end sign when I made the turn. Rallies, postcards, petitions—time-consuming tickets to nowhere. But then what? Elections? In 1964 Lyndon Johnson was the "peace candidate." Then '66, then '68. Who will forget '68? And where were all those congressional peace candidates from Massachusetts today? In six years the electoral process couldn't boast a thimbleful of effective pressure against the war.

But what then? Throw rocks? When I was in the third grade my best friend stole a piece of penny bubble bum from the corner drugstore to show the other kids he wasn't chicken. Just one goddamn piece of bubble gum, but just the same, he couldn't sleep all that night. The next day he put the one-cent haul back on the shelf. He told me the story in tears, and I knew just how he felt. Our conditioning to authority and rules, pernicious as it may sometimes be, was identical. No, it would take a far greater break with my own life's history than I had made thus far to throw a rock.

I stared at the dirty, vibrating floor of the subway. Every now and then the lights were jolted off and we were left for a moment with the darkness of our underground shaft. The subway rumbled and bumbled on.

Above us another act was being played out. Several thousand in the street—some because of an unhappiness and destructiveness that lay within them long before the war, but many others because this was the last, inevitable act in a long and fruitless series of choices. They marched and chanted down Beacon Street to Massachusetts Avenue. There they made the final turn that would take them "all the way." At the bridge across the Charles, the motorcycles and busload of Boston police turned around. The rest of the evening was left to the Cambridge police and state troopers.

"Free Bobby Seale . . . Free Bobby Seale . . . One, two, three, four—we don't want your fucking war!" The chants echoed off the bridge as thousands of trudging feet made their way across the river and into Cambridge. Then they were in front of MIT. The marchers eyed the mammoth complex of buildings where much of the research and design for the war's weapons was carried on. The story upon story of windows were lifeless and mocking. Many of the demonstrators were clinging tightly to the bags of rocks and bottles that they had brought along. "Wait till Harvard Square, wait till Harvard Square," those at the front shouted. The marchers were tense and unsure of themselves. Most had never before been involved in a "trashing."

Then came the word that police ahead had gas equipment. Some who were there mainly out of curiosity broke ranks and decided to go home via another route. Others left temporarily only to find water fountains inside the MIT buildings where they could wet their handkerchiefs, which they could later tie around their faces for gas masks. Most just kept on marching. Then they were at Central Square, and a block farther on they came to the Cambridge City Hall. On the acre of lawn in front of the old stone structure were cordons of police, four men deep, wearing helmets and gas masks. Some held long beige riot sticks, others had tear gas rifles. A couple held carbines. Across the street was another phalanx of police—most of these were straining against the eager German shepherds they held on their leashes. When the marchers came upon this scene they fell deathly silent. The chanting stopped, then the sound of feet was still. A few seconds passed and no one quite knew what to do. Then several at the front yelled, "We're going all the way! All the way to Harvard Square!" Everyone cheered, and the marching and chanting began again. "One, two, three, four—we don't want your fucking war." The cops held nervously to their clubs and rifles and dogs, and watched.

"Harvard Square," the speaker on the subway announced. "Last stop, Harvard Square. Everyone out, please."

I rode the wave of passengers out the car door and up the stairs to the street. The Square was quiet and nearly deserted. The only people around were the older subway passengers, now waiting on the corners of the multiavenued intersection for connecting buses to take them home. The usual denizens of Harvard Square, the young drop-outs, the guitar and recorder players, the spare-change seekers, the underground newspaper salesmen were all gone. Nor could any police be seen. Every day the Square was inhabited by them all, the cops, the "street people," the college radicals. They brushed past each other each day in tensed silence while the business of the stores and banks carried on. The cops gave hard stares at the beads and bell-bottoms and long hair, and the kids glared right back at the dark-blue uniforms and badges. Each could see in the other's face the taut contempt. Every so often one of the cops would say, "Move on, you people," and someone would mutter "Fuckin' pig" below his breath. It wasn't just the couple of weeks that NAC had been planning for the trashing of Harvard Square. This night had been building for years.

I walked a couple of blocks up the nearly soundless Massachusetts Avenue, then turned down a side street toward Leverett House. When I reached my room Marcie had her coat on and was about to leave for a play rehearsal. I took her hand and sat her down next to me on the bed.

"Do you *have* to leave right now?" I asked. She looked away and made the clicking sound of annoyance with her tongue.

"Yes, I *have* to leave right now," she said impatiently. We both looked down at the floor. "Kenny, I'm sorry, I don't like being bitchy but . . . honey, I'm just this way unless I can be on my own without always having to answer to someone. I don't know what I can tell you—you just have to understand." She rose again to leave.

"See you tomorrow?" I asked without looking at her.

"Well no, I have another rehearsal." Her voice became soft again. "I'll give you a call."

"All right. Just be careful and don't go through the Square."

"Don't worry about ol' chicken me," she laughed. "I'll stay miles away." Then she was out the door. I moved over to the window where I sat staring out into Cambridge's blackness. It was as dark and immutable as the subway tunnel. I must have stayed there without moving for half an hour. Not a moving muscle, not a twitch of an emotion. I was feeling nothing. Not physically, not mentally, not anything. I just stared out the window. I felt as though I could stay there for the next sixty years. It was as good a place as any to stay.

Then Bill, the fellow who had moved into Cheyney's old room, came in.

"Hey, Ken, they've gotten to Harvard Square. Let's go down there." Sure, why not, I thought. Curiosity-seeking is bound to be as productive as anything else I've done lately.

"Let me get my coat," I said.

Five minutes later I was standing on a traffic island in the middle of Harvard Square. I've been told that being an onlooker is asking for trouble. At the time, however, I wasn't aware of asking for anything except a good seat and an even better evacuation route. My vantage point allowed me five different streets to choose from in case of a charge. Moreover, I was only a twenty-five-second run from our Moratorium office on Brattle Street. Every two minutes I sank my hand into my pocket and fingered the key to the office's front door.

The marchers were home at last. Three thousand of them

filled the streets and intersections. While some climbed over the locked gates of Harvard Yard and others shinnied up traffic lights, most just stood and walked around, many in small groups, many still clutching at their bags full of rocks. No one seemed quite sure of what would happen next. Four blocks up Mass. Ave., the first busloads of helmeted Cambridge police were moving into formation.

The crowd in the Square was an eclectic bunch. None of the short-haired, SDS Worker-Student Alliance types could be found, since they saw this kind of event as premature and therefore counterproductive to the proletarian cause, but their Weathermen and NAC counterparts were out in full force. Their expressions were grave—furrowed determination to strike a blow at the war and all of capitalism. But for every college-age radical there seemed to be just as many from the twelve-to-sixteen teeny-bopper category. They were smiling and seemingly enjoying this night more than any evening of rebellion in their parents' living room. And although most of the people in the Square were white, many young black kids had joined as well, certainly a far greater percentage than had come to any of the Moratorium rallies. They were trying very hard to make the Panther hope of a white-black, revolutionary coalition a reality.

Clearly, I didn't feel much solidarity with the brigade that surrounded me. Their notions were romantic at best, and thoroughly counterproductive at second best. Some confrontations, usually the type that involve nonviolent resistance, can move people to the left. Everyone can see in those cases which side it is that abuses power. But in these instances, where the demonstrators are clearly and violently the provocateurs, the great silent majority can slide only to the right. But while I felt no affinity for the violent tactics these people sought, I harbored no animosity for them either, at least not *this* night. This night I was too beaten for that.

I tried to imagine what I might do or say if I were given

a platform, a microphone and five minutes to address this crowd. What could I possibly suggest to them as an alternative? I searched my brain, but this night, this April evening of total intellectual and emotional void, I couldn't have bought a single statement to make to them. I let my thoughts meander down every path of logical argument, but every time I was left with the same words thumping against my cranium: "What the fuck?"

I turned to walk down the traffic island a bit to give myself even a little more room from the police when I bumped into another fellow I had been working with in the Moratorium office. "What are *you* doing here?!" we asked simultaneously. I shrugged and he peered over my shoulder at the second wave of cops that was moving out onto Mass. Ave. Then he said, "I don't know. Maybe this is where it's at. Maybe we were just a bunch of dolts and this is the only language the government understands."

"You got me," I said. "These days I don't want to be held to anything I say for more than an hour." He laughed and nodded, and then melted back into the crowd.

Then came a cheer, and I could see that a block away in front of Holyoke Center a group of those younger teeny-boppers had set a trash can on fire and were sitting around it campfire style. But the songs and laughter of the camp and carnival atmosphere were short-lived. Just a minute later the first rock was thrown at Cambridge Trust and the jolting crash of plate glass hitting the cement filled the air. With that sound the last chance to turn back had passed. It was followed by a barrage of thirty more rocks, and every sheet of glass around the bank fell heavily, helplessly to the pavement. For anyone hearing that sound and seeing that sight for the first time it is a frightening, panicking experience that scrambles and splinters all sense. From the time we're little kids we think of banks as the very symbol of indestructible strength—the impenetrable king-

doms of concrete and plate glass and three-foot-thick vault
doors, the place our fathers would bring us along to if we promised to be quiet when we were inside. Seeing a bank fall as
such easy prey is like watching a mammoth ocean liner being
sucked beneath the sea like a popsicle stick. It turns every conditioned expectation topsy-turvy, explodes every inculcated
symbol, and sends a shiver through every cell in the body. It
doesn't matter whether one is for or against the destruction—
the total amazement is the same. Just the sound and sight of
it puts the whole world for that short moment beyond all
prediction and rationality.

With that cue for the confrontation, the police began
marching in tight rows toward the crowd, their riot sticks held
out in front of themselves with both hands. Their boots on the
street made a steady, pounding cadence. Although the sight was
frightful in its military appearance, I knew I was still reasonably
safe as long as the police were only marching. That's their
last nonviolent tactic for clearing a street. It's only when they
charge that the clubs start flying.

Another barrage of rocks was hurled through the night air,
this trajectory, though, in the direction of the police. The
signal was given, and the police began running toward the front
of the crowd. Then the screaming, shouting retreat as the front
lines of the demonstrators were caught from behind and clubbed
to the pavement. Thuds of heavy clubs being rammed into
people's stomachs, and screams from the writhing as their
bones were snapped like twigs. Some of the crying and bleeding
were picked up by the volunteer medics, but most were hoisted
and twisted and shoved into paddy wagons. Like the rest, I fled
from the Square.

Neophyte that I was, I ran along the sidewalk, not even
noticing the store windows at my side that were being smashed
as we ran.

"Get off the sidewalk!" someone shouted, and only then

did I realize that the rocks being hurled from the center of the street were barely missing my head. I went into the middle of the street and kept running until I was out of breath. Then I stopped and sat down on the curb. I had no idea of where any of the people I was with had gone. I sat there, panting and resting for about fifteen minutes. The rear end of the crowd that I was in had thinned out in the retreat. They were now in small groups and walking slowly back toward the Square. No cops could be seen.

I got up and very cautiously started back toward my original position on the traffic island. The police had moved back to *their* original position, but now hundreds more were grouping along various streets leading into the Square. The idea was to pinch the mass of demonstrators in the middle where they could be tear gassed and/or arrested.

In the meantime three banks had been left windowless, and a fourth was in the process of being set afire. Within minutes the smoke and flames were pushing the demonstrators back from the window. Everyone cheered. Ten minutes later the fire trucks came and the protesters left the scene via back streets. I stood unbothered on the traffic island, watching it all. I felt isolated—physically, politically, emotionally. No identification but with self. Not with the cops, not with the violent demonstrators. I was frightened by them both. I could only stand and watch, cynical and yet embarrassed by my curiosity—horrified yet captivated by the emotional upheaval of destruction.

While the police regrouped, the youths that were still in one piece started in on the rest of Harvard Square—the clothing shops, the restaurants, the drugstores, the ice-cream parlors, the camera shops, everything. Within an hour of the first rock not not a window in the several-block area was intact. Unlike the ghetto riots that passed over stores with "Soul Brother" signs, this riot granted immunity to no one. The one business *everyone* seemed eager to trash was the main "hip," "youth culture" clothing store, the one that had sold red strike armbands during the Harvard strike a year before. Regular ones had been a quarter, elastic ones fifty cents. This night its windows were smashed, and on the sidewalk in front someone wrote, "Hip capitalists are also pigs."

When the store fronts were devastated the demonstrators took to the interiors. A fellow with curly blond hair stood in the now open-air display window of Saks Fifth Avenue, which despite its name is on Cambridge's Mount Auburn Street.

"One pair of pants to be liberated," he called to the crowd in front. He held up a pair of pinstriped suit pants, one leg in each hand, and began ripping the clothing into pieces. The crowd cheered. When he reached a tough seam he put one end of the fabric beneath his foot and yanked up. More ripping sound, more little shreds, more cheering. Soon several more climbed through the broken window and helped with the pillaging. On the other side of Mount Auburn St. Harvard's "clubbies" watched through their curtained windows, drinks in their hands and fear in their preppy little hearts. After about five minutes one of the braver and more dapper of them came out and sauntered over to the store.

"Hey, this is good stuff," he said as he picked up a couple of sport jackets and started back toward his club. Everyone booed and one girl snatched the jackets from him, threw them on the sidewalk and lit them with a match. Another hippier type, who had also draped clothes over his shoulder, was similarly relieved of his spoils. "Destroy but don't loot" was the moment's moral code. Shortly after that, however, a young black high school kid also decided to loot. He walked into the store, piled several suits and coats over his arms, and walked out with a smile. The white radicals stood by, at first silent then shouting, "Right on!" Heavens, no one there wanted to be *racist!*

With that precedent the mass looting began. One store

after another, goods being carried out by whites, blacks, club-bies, hippies, radicals, nearly everyone. It was the final logical step in this night without logic.

But the despoilers hadn't much time. Hundreds more police had been brought in, and the final, penetrating sweep of the Square began. With billows of tear gas clearing the way, the cops marched in from all directions. At first I thought I would be trapped on my cement island, but then saw that part of Brattle Street was still clear. With my eyes burning and tearing from the gas, I ran with the rest of the frightened herd. A few turned around so they were facing the fleeing mob and shouted, "Don't run, walk. Keep calm and walk." I was too riled and afraid to even consider the merits of the suggestion. I kept on running, my heart pounding. Just ahead and to the right club swinging cops were coming up Church Street. Every-one was on his own. Muffled blasts of tear-gas canisters, screams of those who couldn't get out of the way of clubs, but mostly all I could hear was my own heaving breath. Finally, just before the cops made it onto Brattle Street, I reached the Moratorium office. With one last, insane look at the cops, who were now maybe thirty yards away, the streetlights glaring off their blue helmets and translucent face shields, I headed for the front door. It was already open. I never looked back again, just raced up the stairs to the third floor.

When I got to the top I found Rich, our press secretary, sitting at the reception desk typing away. Except for the small Tensor lamp at his side, the office suite was completely dark-ened. He looked up and in the dim light I could see his expres-sion of terror before realizing who I was.

"Don't panic, Rich, it's only me." He leaned back in his chair and slumped his shoulders in relief.

"Whew! I thought for sure this was going to be a Chicago McCarthy headquarters all over again." I looked at the wall directly behind him—it was covered with our antiwar posters, and I shuddered, just imagining the scene if the cops were to come up here.

"I'm typing up a disclaimer here condemning the violence," he said. "Want to read it?"

I didn't answer as I walked into an adjoining room and without daring to turn on a light sat down at my desk. At first it appeared completely black and I couldn't even see my own fingers before me. But then after a minute or so my eyes adjusted and the small, silver rectangle of light that was shoved through the window and branded on the wooden floor was enough for me to pick out the objects around me. I began thumbing through all the familiar sheets and cards on my desk. Names and addresses of campus coordinators, old phone messages, the original press release announcing the April 15 rally, graphic designs, and tons more of useless, history-trampled paper. A lot of silt left behind by a spring downpour.

Through the wall came the rat-a-tat-tat of Rich's electric tyupewriter. "Good sailor, Rich," I thought. "Keep typing 'till the last tip of railing on our stern is underwater." Outside were more blunted blasts of tear-gas canisters, and in the distance more muffled tinkling of broken glass. I went cautiously to the window and looked out. Being in a dark room, I could stand at the window without being seen by anyone of the street, indeed a favorable advantage. It was like looking through a one-way mirror. For several blocks in front of me and to both sides I could see it all—cops searching down one street, kids retreating through an alleyway, cops sneaking up from behind and firing tear gas, demonstrators sneaking up from behind and throwing rocks.

For a moment I felt as though it were my own little game. I knew everything about them and they knew nothing about me. I stood above it all, invisible, and they were all my little players. I could tilt and rearrange however I pleased. Put half a dozen cops here and twenty demonstrators over there and see what happens. Then move them around and see if it makes a difference, if it makes the game any more exciting. Perhaps be even *really* innovative and give the kids the clubs and rifles and the cops the rocks and bottles. I wonder then who would be for and who would be against the war. Who would chant and who would move to a march drill? Then give the clubs and rifles back to the cops, but give the "legitimate authority" of the state to the kids. Who then would be the *demonstrators*? Would the stores and capitalism be allies or enemies of the state? It was all great fun and intrigue. How many permutations of American society could I construct? Would any of them make any difference? Or is the society immutably chained by clashing roles where someone always has a little more power and someone else a little less? I pushed and shoved at the game, switching the ages, the uniforms, the beliefs, eventually everything, and it all seemed to make no ultimate difference.

I recoiled from the play and was again plain, frightened me, hiding in an office where I could stand and control as a spectator. But could I really? I laughed at myself for such thoughts. I could stand there and watch it all, that's true, but control? No, I had none of that. The cops looked and believed and moved the way cops always look and believe and move, and the same for the demonstrators. No, this game wasn't terribly much fun. I had no control at all.

"Hey, what are you looking at?" Rich asked as he came up from behind. He joined me at the window. "Zow, quite a view." He then began lifting the window very cautiously, very quietly. But he wasn't as deft as he thought, and a cop just below swivelled around into a squat, and pointed his carbine right at our faces.

"Get your goddamn heads out of the window," he shouted. Rich closed the window and we both sank into chairs, only then realizing how close we had come to a very foolish end. We sat there for several minutes without speaking, just listening to the sounds of a writhing society outside our window. Then Rich went back to work and when he finished he left via the back exit for home.

I began cleaning out my desk, discarding most in the wastebasket and sticking a few of my personal belongings inside my jacket. I wouldn't be coming back to the office after tonight. When I finished I sat quietly in the dark room, waiting. For nearly an hour I stared at the streetlight just outside the window. Then it was deathly quiet. I went to the window and saw that on every corner small groups of cops were standing around, talking and relaxing, their gas masks back on their belts. No demonstrators could be seen. Hundreds had been arrested, scores were being treated in hospitals.

I went slowly down the stairs and came out the front door. As I began down the sidewalk toward Leverett House I could feel the cops' stares and hatred reverberating all around me.

"Why don't you give him a little help?" one of the cops in a squad car called to another across the street who was holding on to a hundred pound German shepherd. I quickened my pace and their laughter rolled out like a drool. All the way home cops lined the streets, telling the few passersby there would be a curfew in another hour. I kept my hands in my pockets and my eyes straight ahead. After ten paranoid minutes I was back inside the gates of Leverett House. A few fellows I knew were standing around the elevators, exchanging riot stories and comparing bruised shoulders. I stepped between them and into the elevator.

"Well, did you learn anything down at the Square tonight?" one of them asked me.

"Yeah, *Casablanca's* coming to the Brattle Theater this Friday." Then I let the elevator doors slide shut.

When I pushed open the door to my room I found it dark and empty. As she said she would, Marcie had gone directly back to Wellesley from her play rehearsal. A book she had forgotten lay on the couch. I took off my jacket and discovered the two leaflets from the rally were still wedged in the pockets. I laid them on the windowsill in front of me, and with an unusually intense desire for perfection, began folding them into two remarkably streamlined paper airplanes. Like riding a bicycle, it's something one just doesn't forget how to do. With the light still off I opened up one of the side windows and looked down at the empty street below. Although I'm rarely a litterbug, it was nothing more or less than pure compulsion that twice cocked my wrist and sent those missiles gliding out and down into the darkness. I cheered their poised performance, closed the window, and went to bed.

Almost all of that last week in April, it seems, I spent most of my time just walking around. But the most one can hope for from old haunts is perhaps a slightly new look that will keep the mind off the past. Certainly Harvard Square had a new look, but it was the deadened, condemned look of plywood over storefronts. Everything was boarded up. Behind the graffitied wooden barriers, outraged businessmen began planning ways in which they could organize against the radical community, while outside the same cops, hippies, and radicals again brushed past each other in their daylight roles, each knowing that the other had been there that night and that soon they would probably all meet again under similar circumstances.

To be sure, the inside of the Yard was a more palatable sight. There the spring was coaxing the reluctant bushes and branches back to life, the air was washed with the scent of lilacs, and dozens of young couples were again bringing their books out to study on the steps of Widener Library or beneath

the trees in front of Memorial Church. Harvard's grounds-
keepers were also out in full battalion, already preparing the
acreage for commencement exercises. They seemed to be trying
harder than ever to preen the grass and ivy to a heightened
greenness that would make the endowing alumni think more
of what was the same rather than of what had changed in their
old campus community.

As I walked by myself from one end of the campus to the
other, over and over again, I tried as best I could to sort out
all the confusion that made my wanderings so aimless. Politically, my first reactions were sour and resentful. That part of
my life over the last year, much like my first love affair, had
been one sailing romantic leap. And now I was at the bottom
of the fall and convinced I was through with it for good. It
all comes to nothing, I told myself. Ultimately nothing changes.
Politics is a time trap, I said, that whittles a life away like a
terminal disease. Not for me. I'll be a writer, and if I worry
about anything, it will be over the few close relationships in my
life which I have *some* control over. That's what I said.

During my week's wanderings I ran into many of the
people I had worked with in Boston on the Moratorium. Most
seemed to be feeling the same way. Like everyone else our age,
they were of course still suffering from the tension between personal longings and the proverbial "social conscience," but now
they too were tending toward the personal pursuits. Some had
dropped out of politics completely. No faith in working within
the system; yet too repelled by violence to work outside of it.
"Student activism," one of them said, "is going on a long
vacation."

But no matter how many times I told myself I was finished
with trying to change the world and that from now on I would
try only to keep the world from changing me, I never seemed
fully able to repress the other side of me, the side that craved
to get on the phone again and start all over. And thus, with

the invasion of Cambodia in May, I again found myself hammering away at our government. I even decided to try new chan-
nels such as civil disobedience. Along with two hundred others
I marched down to Boston Army Base to block passage to the
buses that were carrying new inductees. But still I was ambivalent and questioning my actions. Was I really aiding the
antiwar movement or was I just some middle-class college kid
trying to prove to himself his willingness to go to jail? Was I
being effective or only cathartic? The uncertainty continued to
gnaw.

Although it seemed I had barely resigned from politics
and already I was back again dialing those numbers and inking
the mimeo, it wasn't quite as *déjà vu* as all that. This time
around I could sense within me a certain mellowness, a certain
realism in my expectations, a certain contact between my feet
and the ground. We weren't going to end the war in a week,
and we weren't even about to completely reverse the new policy
in Cambodia, but we were going to continue building pressure
toward both ends. And most importantly, we were going to use
the opportunity to continue educating Americans to the doom
of any society that bases its strength on aggressive militarism.

And of course, that word, education, that arduous, unro-
mantic task of changing people's opinions is the obvious, yet
rebuffed key to it all. Far too many of us younger souls who
flirt with political activism recognize education as the basis of
change, but at the same time recoil from the actual task. Instead we too often opt for the more exciting and immediately
visible activities like rally organizing or electioneering every two
or four years.

Throughout that revitalized May, these few simple recogni-
tions became clear. Although our press releases always stated
that we had given the president a "mandate" and that we
weren't being listened to, the simple fact of the matter was that
the "silent majority" Nixon referred to was an actuality. No

matter how many millions we were able to draw to marches and rallies, the population of this country remained *two hundred* million, and the majority was his.

If we are to remain committed to majority rule, it then seems clear what our futures must be all about. It won't be a token two hours of canvassing twice a year that wins over the majority. On the war issue as well as every other social issue in the future, it's going to take daily, monthly, yearly work that must somehow be integrated into our lives' other pursuits. In its most unglorious terms, this means a certain amount of time every day or week or month, not just reinforcing our own beliefs but instead dealing with that giant, amorphous middle-America. If we are unable to accept these few realities, the course of student activism faces only two alternatives—acceptance of the radicals' belief in imposing upon and coercing the majority, and the deluding panacea that justifies it; or the manic depressions of political romanticism that can drive us all from ever attempting to change anything.

These simple facts seemed and continue to seem true to me. Over a year's time I came to realize the injury that comes with untempered romanticism. But whether or not I can change my own approach still turns me in my sleep. I simply don't know yet whether I can forge the idealism needed to begin with the realism needed to finish, whether I can combine a personal life and nonpolitical career with the contact I feel I must keep with the political movements of the future. Somehow the questions and doubts never lie down and surrender. Every day the tranquil agreement of yesterday is destroyed. That's when I bury myself in a coat and go for a walk. And I walk and walk until it seems I've rid myself of it all, until all the past and the doubts and the second guessing have left. Only then, when I feel voided and indifferent to my own vacillating judgments, do I turn the corner for home.